TEACHER'S MANUAL AND ACHIEVEMENT TESTS

NORTHSTAR 1
LISTENING AND SPEAKING

SECOND EDITION

AUTHORS
Polly Merdinger
Laurie Barton

SERIES EDITORS
Frances Boyd
Carol Numrich

PEARSON
Longman

NorthStar: Listening and Speaking Level 1, Second Edition
Teacher's Manual and Achievement Tests

Pearson Education, 10 Bank Street, White Plains, NY 10606

Teacher's Manual by Robin Mills. Activities for secondary schools by Ann Hilborn and Linda Riehl.

Achievement Tests developed by Dr. Joan Jamieson and Dr. Carol Chapelle.

Achievement Tests by Tony Becker, Maja Grgurovic, Elizabeth Henly, and Dana Klinek.

Staff credits: The people who made up the *NorthStar: Listening and Speaking Level 1, Second Edition Teacher's Manual* team, representing editorial, production, design, and manufacturing, are Dave Dickey, Christine Edmonds, Ann France, Gosia Jaros-White, Dana Klinek, Melissa Leyva, Sherry Preiss, Robert Ruvo, Debbie Sistino, Jennifer Stem, and Paula Van Ells.

Cover Art: Silvia Rojas/Getty Images
Text composition: ElectraGraphics, Inc.
Text font: 11.5/13 Minion

ISBN-10: 0-13-613336-3
ISBN-13: 978-0-13-613336-0

PEARSON LONGMAN ON THE WEB

Pearsonlongman.com offers online resources for teachers and students. Access our Companion Websites, our online catalog, and our local offices around the world.

Visit us at **www.pearsonlongman.com**.

Printed in the United States of America
1 2 3 4 5 6 7 8 9 10—HAM—13 12 11 10 09 08

CONTENTS

Welcome to *NorthStar*, Second Edition iv
Overview of the Teacher's Manual
    and Achievement Tests xiv

UNIT-BY-UNIT TEACHING SUGGESTIONS

UNIT 1   **Faraway Friends** I

UNIT 2   **Recycled Fashion** 12

UNIT 3   **Rap Music** 23

UNIT 4   **Something Valuable** 34

UNIT 5   **Together Is Better** 45

UNIT 6   **Thinking Young: Creativity in Business** 56

UNIT 7   **Planting Trees for Peace** 67

UNIT 8   **Driving You Crazy** 78

UNIT 9   **Only Child—Lonely Child?** 89

UNIT 10   **The Beautiful Game** 99

      Student Book Answer Key 109
      Unit Word List 120

ACHIEVEMENT TESTS

UNIT 1   . . . . T-I

UNIT 2   . . . . T-7

UNIT 3   . . . . T-12

UNIT 4   . . . . T-19

UNIT 5   . . . . T-25

UNIT 6   . . . . T-30

UNIT 7   . . . . T-36

UNIT 8   . . . . T-42

UNIT 9   . . . . T-47

UNIT 10   . . . . T-53

      Achievement Tests Audioscript T-59
      Achievement Tests Answer Key T-68

WELCOME TO NORTHSTAR

SECOND EDITION

NorthStar, now in its new edition, motivates students to succeed in their **academic** as well as **personal** language goals.

For each of the five levels, the two strands—*Reading and Writing* and *Listening and Speaking*—provide a fully integrated approach for students and teachers.

WHAT IS SPECIAL ABOUT THE NEW EDITION?

NEW THEMES

New themes and **updated content**—presented in a **variety of genres**, including literature and lectures, and in **authentic reading and listening selections**—challenge students intellectually.

ACADEMIC SKILLS

More purposeful **integration of critical thinking** and an enhanced focus on **academic skills** such as inferencing, synthesizing, note taking, and test taking help students develop strategies for **success** in the **classroom** and on **standardized tests**. A **culminating productive task** galvanizes content, language, and **critical thinking skills**.

➤ In the *Listening and Speaking* strand, a **structured approach** gives students opportunities for **more extended and creative oral practice**, for example, presentations, simulations, debates, case studies, and public service announcements.

➤ In the *Reading and Writing* strand, a new, **fully integrated writing section** leads students through the **writing process** with engaging writing assignments focusing on various rhetorical modes.

NEW DESIGN

Full **color pages** with more **photos, illustrations, and graphic organizers** foster student engagement and make the content and activities come alive.

MyNorthStarLab

MyNorthStarLab, an easy-to-use **online learning and assessment program**, offers:

➤ Unlimited access to reading and listening selections and DVD segments.

➤ Focused test preparation to help students succeed on international exams such as TOEFL® and IELTS®. Pre- and post-unit assessments improve results by providing individualized instruction, instant feedback, and personalized study plans.

➤ Original activities that support and extend the *NorthStar* program. These include pronunciation practice using voice recording tools, and activities to build note taking skills and academic vocabulary.

➤ Tools that save time. These include a flexible gradebook and authoring features that give teachers control of content and help them track student progress.

THE NORTHSTAR APPROACH

The *NorthStar* series is based on **current research in language acquisition** and on the **experiences of teachers and curriculum designers**. Five principles guide the *NorthStar* approach.

PRINCIPLES

1 The more profoundly students are stimulated intellectually and emotionally, the more language they will use and retain.

The thematic organization of *NorthStar* promotes intellectual and emotional stimulation. The 50 sophisticated themes in *NorthStar* present intriguing topics such as recycled fashion, restorative justice, personal carbon footprints, and microfinance. The authentic content engages students, links them to language use outside of the classroom, and encourages personal expression and critical thinking.

2 Students can learn both the form and content of the language.

Grammar, vocabulary, and culture are inextricably woven into the units, providing students with systematic and multiple exposures to language forms in a variety of contexts. As the theme is developed, students can express complex thoughts using a higher level of language.

3 Successful students are active learners.

Tasks are designed to be creative, active, and varied. Topics are interesting and up-to-date. Together these tasks and topics (1) allow teachers to bring the outside world into the classroom and (2) motivate students to apply their classroom learning in the outside world.

4 Students need feedback.

This feedback comes naturally when students work together practicing language and participating in open-ended opinion and inference tasks. Whole class activities invite teachers' feedback on the spot or via audio/video recordings or notes. The innovative new MyNorthStarLab gives students immediate feedback as they complete computer-graded language activities online; it also gives students the opportunity to submit writing or speaking assignments electronically to their instructor for feedback later.

5 The quality of relationships in the language classroom is important because students are asked to express themselves on issues and ideas.

The information and activities in *NorthStar* promote genuine interaction, acceptance of differences, and authentic communication. By building skills and exploring ideas, the exercises help students participate in discussions and write essays of an increasingly complex and sophisticated nature.

THE NorthStar UNIT

① FOCUS ON THE TOPIC

This section introduces students to the unifying theme
of the listening selections.

> **PREDICT** and **SHARE INFORMATION** foster interest in the unit topic and help
> students develop a personal connection to it.
>
> **BACKGROUND** AND **VOCABULARY** activities provide students with tools for
> understanding the first listening selection. Later in the unit, students review
> this vocabulary and learn related idioms, collocations, and word forms. This
> helps them explore content and expand their written and spoken language.

UNIT
6

Thinking Young:
Creativity in Business

Picture 1

Picture 2

①FOCUS ON THE TOPIC

Ⓐ PREDICT

Look at the pictures. Discuss the questions with the class.

1. What are the co-workers doing in picture 1? How do they feel?
2. What are the same co-workers doing in picture 2? How do they feel?
3. What does "Thinking Young" mean?

101

Ⓑ SHARE INFORMATION

Creative people have new and unusual ideas. Sometimes they create or make
new things. Children are usually creative when they play. They have many
new ideas.

1 *When you were a child, what creative thing(s) did you do? Circle your answers.
Then share your answers with three classmates. Ask, "What did you do?"*

a. I created a new game or toy.

b. I created a piece of art (painting, sculpture).

c. I wrote a song or played a musical instrument.

d. I wrote a story or poem.

e. I solved a problem in an unusual way.

f. (something else?) _____

2 *When you were creative, how did you feel? Circle all the words that describe your
feelings. Use your dictionary for help.*

a. proud

b. excited

c. happy

d. nervous

e. (another feeling?) _____

Ⓒ BACKGROUND AND VOCABULARY

1 🎧 *Read and listen to the information from the business magazine Fast
Company.*

> ### Can Your Employees Learn to Be More Creative?
> ## Many Business Owners Say "YES!"
>
> Big companies, like American Express®, Microsoft®, FedEx
> Kinko's®, and Disney®, want their **employees** to be creative—to
> think in new and interesting ways. These companies pay billions
> of dollars for **creativity** classes for their employees.

102   UNIT 6

② FOCUS ON LISTENING

This section focuses on understanding two contrasting listening selections.

LISTENING ONE is a radio report, interview, lecture, or other genre that addresses the unit topic. In levels 1 to 3, listenings are based on authentic materials. In levels 4 and 5, all the listenings are authentic.

LISTEN FOR MAIN IDEAS and **LISTEN FOR DETAILS** are comprehension activities that lead students to an understanding and appreciation of the first selection.

The **MAKE INFERENCES** activity prompts students to "listen between the lines," move beyond the literal meaning, exercise critical thinking skills, and understand the listening on a more academic level. Students follow up with pair or group work to discuss topics in the **EXPRESS OPINIONS** section.

---

② FOCUS ON LISTENING

Ⓐ LISTENING ONE: Hello. This is the Friendship Force.

Nina and Rick are talking about the Friendship Force. Listen to the beginning of the conversation. Then answer the questions.

1. What are you listening to? Check (✓) the answer.
   _____ a telephone call   _____ a radio talk show

2. What will Nina and Rick talk about? Check (✓) your ideas.

   _____ host families   _____ shopping   _____ traveling
   _____ hotels   _____ music   _____ groups
   _____ students   _____ children   _____ languages

◖LISTEN FOR MAIN IDEAS

1 *Listen to the conversation between Nina and Rick. Read the sentences. Write **T** (true) or **F** (false).*

   _____ 1. Friendship Force visitors can be young or old.

   _____ 2. Some Friendship Force visitors stay in hotels.

   _____ 3. Nina wants to stay with a host family in Thailand.

   _____ 4. All host families speak English.

   _____ 5. Nina and Rick agree that it's good to have international friends.

2 *Go back to Section 2A, Question 2. Were your answers correct?*

◖LISTEN FOR DETAILS

Listen again. Circle the correct answer to complete each sentence.

1. Each group has _____ people.
   a. 13 to 50   **b.** 15 to 30

2. Friendship Force groups meet for the first time _____.
   a. before they travel   **b.** in the new country

3. Nina thinks that when you live with a host family, you learn _____.
   a. their language   **b.** about their country

4. Nina _____ Thai (the language of Thailand).
   a. speaks a little   **b.** doesn't speak

---

5. Friendship Force visitors stay with their host families for two _____.
   a. weeks   **b.** months

6. After they stay with their host family, many Friendship Force visitors travel _____.
   a. to a different country **b.** in the same country

7. Nina will get an application for the Friendship Force _____.
   a. from Rick   **b.** on the Internet

◖MAKE INFERENCES

Listen to the excerpts from Listening One. Circle the correct answer to complete each sentence.

Excerpt One

1. Nina is probably a _____ student.
   a. high school   **b.** college

Excerpt Two

2. Nina is probably a _____ person.
   a. nervous   **b.** friendly

Excerpt Three

3. Nina doesn't speak Thai. She is asking Rick, "Will I _____?"
   a. have problems   **b.** learn the language

Excerpt Four

4. "People, not places" means, "You learn more about a new country when you _____."
   a. meet the people   **b.** visit the important places

◖EXPRESS OPINIONS

Discuss the questions with the class.

1. Do you think it's good to stay with a host family? Why or why not?

2. Do you need to speak the same language well to make friends with someone? Why or why not?

3. What are the best ways to learn about another country?

LISTENING TWO offers another perspective on the topic and is usually another genre. Again, in levels 1 to 3, the listenings are based on authentic materials and in levels 4 and 5, they are authentic. This second listening is followed by an activity that challenges students to question ideas they formed about the first listening, and to use appropriate language skills to analyze and explain their ideas.

INTEGRATE LISTENINGS ONE AND TWO presents culminating activities. Students are challenged to take what they have learned, organize the information, and synthesize it in a meaningful way. Students practice skills that are essential for success in authentic academic settings and on standardized tests.

---

4. I don't like to spend money on clothing. I don't think it's necessary to spend a lot of money on pants or a dress.

_____ Agree

_____ Disagree

5. I want to be a fashion designer. I think making new clothes is very exciting.

_____ Agree

_____ Disagree

B LISTENING TWO: The Quilts of Gee's Bend

Gee's Bend is the name of a small town in Alabama. The women of Gee's Bend are famous for their quilts. They use old materials to make beautiful quilts.

C INTEGRATE LISTENINGS ONE AND TWO

◀ STEP 1: Organize

Answer the questions in the chart. Use information from Listenings One and Two.

USING RECYCLED MATERIALS		
	Deborah Lindquist	**Gee's Bend Women**
1. What do they do?	Makes trendy clothes with unusual materials; makes eco-fashion	
2. Why do they use recycled materials?		
3. Where do they live?		

◀ STEP 2: Synthesize

Imagine that Deborah Lindquist from Listening One and the Gee's Bend woman from Listening Two are speaking to a news reporter.

1 *Role-play. Work in groups of three. Complete the conversation with information from Step 1: Organize.*

REPORTER: What do you make?
LINDQUIST: I make . . .
GEE'S BEND WOMAN: Well, I don't make . . .
REPORTER: Why do you use recycled materials?
GEE'S BEND WOMAN: I use them because . . .
LINDQUIST: I use recycled materials . . .

2 *Practice responding to the questions. Then share one question and the answer with the class.*

---

③ FOCUS ON SPEAKING

This section emphasizes development of productive skills for speaking. It includes sections on vocabulary, grammar, pronunciation, functional language, and an extended speaking task.

> The **VOCABULARY** section leads students from reviewing the unit vocabulary, to practicing and expanding their use of it, and then working with it—using it creatively in both this section and in the final speaking task.
>
> Students learn useful structures for speaking in the **GRAMMAR** section, which offers a concise presentation and targeted practice. Vocabulary items are recycled here, providing multiple exposures leading to mastery. For additional practice with the grammar presented, students and teachers can consult the GRAMMAR BOOK REFERENCES at the end of the book for corresponding material in the *Focus on Grammar* and Azar series.

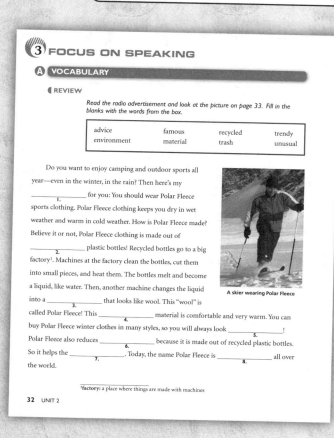

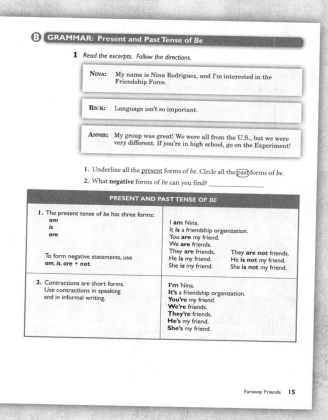

The **PRONUNCIATION** section presents both controlled and freer, communicative practice of the sounds and patterns of English. Models from the listening selections reinforce content and vocabulary. This is followed by the **FUNCTION** section where students are exposed to functional language that prepares them to express ideas on a higher level. Examples have been chosen based on frequency, variety, and usefulness for the final speaking task.

The **PRODUCTION** section gives students an opportunity to integrate the ideas, vocabulary, grammar, pronunciation, and function presented in the unit. This final speaking task is the culminating activity of the unit and gets students to exchange ideas and express opinions in sustained speaking contexts. Activities are presented in a sequence that builds confidence and fluency, and allows for more than one "try" at expression. When appropriate, students practice some presentation skills: audience analysis, organization, eye contact, or use of visuals.

C SPEAKING

◀ **PRONUNCIATION** of *TH: think, this*

How many words with "th" can you find in this sentence?

We sold 333,333 pairs of Wristies.

PRONOUNCING *TH* SOUNDS

Put the tip of your tongue between your teeth.

This is the most important part of the pronunciation of the "th" sounds.

Blow out air to make the sound. Keep the tip of your tongue between your teeth.

The "th" sound in *this, these,* and *then* is a voiced sound. The vocal cords vibrate.
The "th" sound in *think, three,* and *thousand* is a voiceless sound. The vocal cords do not vibrate.

The tip of the tongue is between the teeth for both sounds.

1 *Read the sentences and underline every word that has a "th" sound. Then read the sentences aloud to a partner. Be sure to pronounce all the "th" sounds correctly. Listen to the sentences to check your pronunciation.*

1. They're long gloves with no fingers.

2. There's a hole for the thumb.

3. Some people wear them outside; others wear them inside.

4. They all wore them every day.

5. So then I thought, "I can sell these things!"

6. My mother didn't know anything about business.

7. A lot of stores sell them, and there's also a website.

◀ **PRODUCTION: Role-Play**

In this unit, you learned about three important women—Wangari Maathai, Rigoberta Menchu, and Eleanor Roosevelt. *In this activity, you are going to play the role of one of these women.* Try to use the vocabulary, grammar, pronunciation, and language for expressing similarities from the unit.*

Step 1: Divide the class into three groups: Group A—Wangari Maathai, Group B—Rigoberta Menchu, and Group C—Eleanor Roosevelt.

Step 2: As a group, talk about your person's life. Be sure that every student in the group knows all the information. Look back at the unit to check any information you need. Then write four questions that your person can ask the other two important women about their lives. Every person in the group must write all four questions.

Step 3: Make new groups with at least one person from Group A, Group B, and Group C. Take turns telling about "your" life (as Wangari, Rigoberta, or Eleanor). Use "I . . ." Answer any questions that your partners ask you.

When your partners are speaking, listen very carefully. If one person tells about an experience, and you had the same experience, tell him/her immediately, using "too" or "either".

*For Alternative Speaking Topics, see page 146.

ALTERNATIVE SPEAKING TOPICS are provided at the end of the unit. They can be used as alternatives to the final speaking task, or as *additional* assignments. RESEARCH TOPICS tied to the theme of the unit are organized in a special section at the back of the book.

MyNorthStarLab

MyNorthStarLab supports students with **individualized instruction, feedback,** and **extra help.** A wide array of resources, including a flexible **gradebook,** helps teachers manage student progress.

The MyNorthStarLab **WELCOME** page **organizes assignments and grades,** and **facilitates communication** between students and teachers.

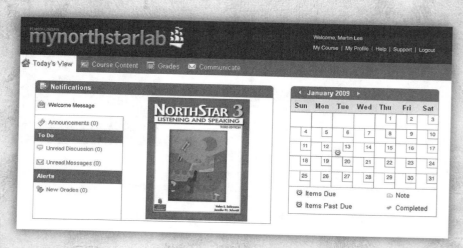

For each unit, MyNorthStarLab provides a **READINESS CHECK.**

➤ Activities **assess** student knowledge **before** beginning the unit and **follow up** with individualized instruction.

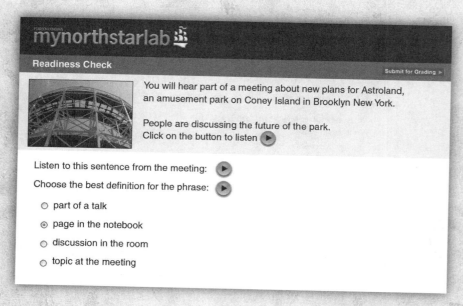

Student book material and **new** practice activities are available to students online.

➤ Students benefit from virtually unlimited **practice anywhere, anytime**.

Interaction with **Internet** and **video** materials will:

➤ Expand students' knowledge of the topic.

➤ Help students practice new vocabulary and grammar.

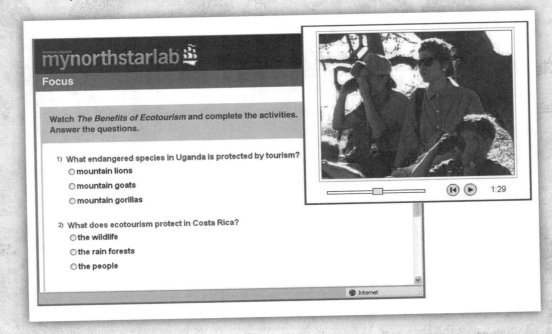

INTEGRATED SKILL ACTIVITIES in MyNorthStarLab challenge students to bring together the **language skills** and **critical thinking skills** that they have practiced throughout the unit.

The MyNorthStarLab **ASSESSMENT** tools allow instructors to customize and deliver achievement tests online.

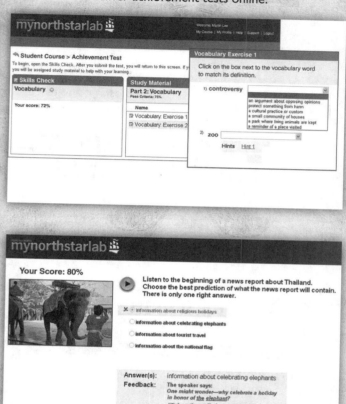

THE ADVENTURE OF A LIFETIME

We at the Antarctic Travel Society encourage you to consider an excited guided tour of Antarctica for your next vacation.

The Antarctic Travel society carefully plans and operates tours of the Antarctic by ship. There are three trips per day leaving from ports in South America and Australia. Each ship carries only about 100 passengers at a time. Tours run from November through March to the ice-free areas along the coast of Antarctica.

In addition to touring the coast, our ships stop for on-land visits, which generally last for about three hours. Activities include guided sightseeing, mountain climbing, camping, kayaking, and scuba diving. For a longer stay, camping trips can also be arranged.

Our tours will give you an opportunity to experience the richness of Antarctica, including its wildlife, history, active research stations, and, most of all, its natural beauty.

Tours are supervised by the ship's staff. The staff generally includes experts in animal and sea life and other Antarctica specialists. There is generally one staff member for every 10 to 20 passengers. Theses trained and responsible individuals will help to make your visit to Antarctica safe, educational, and unforgettable.

READ, LISTEN AND WRITE ABOUT TOURISM IN ANTARCTICA
Read.
Read the text. Then answer the question.

According to the text, how can tourism benefit the Antartic?

Listen.
Click on the Play button and listen to the passage.
Use the outline to take notes as you listen.

Main idea:

Seven things that scientists study:

The effects of tourism:

Write.
Write about the potential and risks in Antarctica.
Follow the steps to prepare.

Step 1
• Review the text and your outline from the listening task.
• Write notes about the benefits and risks of tourism.

Step 2
Write for 20 minutes. Leave 5 minutes to edit your work.

OVERVIEW OF THE TEACHER'S MANUAL AND ACHIEVEMENT TESTS

The **NorthStar Teacher's Manual** includes:

➤ Specific suggestions for teaching each unit

➤ Student Book Answer Key

➤ An alphabetized-by-unit word list of the key vocabulary items practiced in each unit

➤ Reproducible Achievement Tests with Answer Keys—including the test audioscript and test audio CD

UNIT-BY-UNIT TEACHING SUGGESTIONS

Unit-by-unit overview (scope and sequence), list of skills practiced in each section of the student book, suggested teaching times, teaching suggestions, suggestions on how to use *NorthStar* in secondary classes, Expansion/Homework activities, cross-references to the companion strand, techniques and instructions for using MyNorthStarLab

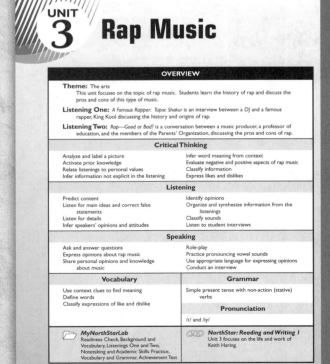

UNIT 3 Rap Music

OVERVIEW

Theme: The arts
This unit focuses on the topic of rap music. Students learn the history of rap and discuss the pros and cons of this type of music.

Listening One: *A Famous Rapper: Tupac Shakur* is an interview between a DJ and a famous rapper, King Kool discussing the history and origins of rap.

Listening Two: *Rap—Good or Bad?* is a conversation between a music producer, a professor of education, and the members of the Parents' Organization, discussing the pros and cons of rap.

Critical Thinking

Analyze and label a picture	Infer word meaning from context
Activate prior knowledge	Evaluate negative and positive aspects of rap music
Relate listenings to personal values	Classify information
Infer information not explicit in the listening	Express likes and dislikes

Listening

Predict content	Identify opinions
Listen for main ideas and correct false statements	Organize and synthesize information from the listenings
Listen for details	Classify sounds
Infer speakers' opinions and attitudes	Listen to student interviews

Speaking

Ask and answer questions	Role-play
Express opinions about rap music	Practice pronouncing vowel sounds
Share personal opinions and knowledge about music	Use appropriate language for expressing opinions
	Conduct an interview

Vocabulary / Grammar

Vocabulary	Grammar
Use context clues to find meaning	Simple present tense with non-action (stative) verbs
Define words	
Classify expressions of like and dislike	**Pronunciation**
	/ɪ/ and /iy/

MyNorthStarLab	NorthStar: Reading and Writing 1
Readiness Check, Background and Vocabulary, Listenings One and Two, Notetaking and Academic Skills Practice, Vocabulary and Grammar, Achievement Test	Unit 3 focuses on the life and work of Keith Haring.

23

unfamiliar, have students underline them. Go over students' questions before they complete the next exercise.

2. Have students work in pairs to complete **Exercise 2**. Encourage them to point to the place in the text where the answers can be found. When done, go over the answers as a class.

3. Have students complete **Exercise 3**. Start by going over pronunciation of the words in the box. As you pronounce the words, write them on the board. Have students mark out syllables and stress of each word as you mark them on the board. Go over the answers as a class.

Go to www.mynorthstarlab.com for additional *Background and Vocabulary* practice.

②FOCUS ON LISTENING

◖ **SKILLS**

Predict content; identify main ideas; listen for details; make inferences; express opinions; listen to a conversation and identify opinions.

°°°Ⓐ **LISTENING ONE: A Famous Rapper: Tupac Shakur**

Go to www.mynorthstarlab.com to listen to *A Famous Rapper: Tupac Shakur.*

Suggested Time: 5 minutes

Listening One is a radio interview with rapper King Kool about the history of rap and a famous rapper, Tupac Shakur. The conversational style is informal.

1. Have students listen to the beginning of the conversation and answer the questions. Encourage students to take notes.

2. Go over the answers as a class. Explain to students that their answers are just predictions and they will find out if they were correct after listening to the whole interview.

LISTENING STRATEGY: Listening Guides

1. In order to set a purpose for listening, provide students with a framework or guide. Tell students that a guide for listening can help them focus on the task. As a whole group, develop questions to use in a guide. For example, *What do I know about the topic? What do I expect to find out? Who is the speaker? What is the main idea of the interview? What information is presented about the topic?*

2. Following the audio, allow time for students to discuss and demonstrate an understanding of the material. Extend the lesson by assigning students the task of writing an informative paragraph on the topic using the newly acquired information.

Rap Music 25

USING *NORTHSTAR* IN SECONDARY CLASSES

Each unit of the *Teacher's Manual* offers a set of strategies that provide opportunities for greater differentiation in a typical mixed classroom to meet the needs of multi-level secondary students. These strategies are equally beneficial in academic and adult classes. The scaffolded instruction enables teachers to facilitate student mastery of complex skills and ideas. Repeated exposure to concepts helps accelerate English language learning.

Reading/Listening Strategies give teachers additional support to guide students who have limited experience with basic reading/listening skills as they learn to explore and understand academic content. Suggestions are given to help students understand how to predict, determine main idea and supporting details, navigate and comprehend a text, monitor their understanding, and organize information.

Reaching All Students are activity suggestions for two levels of language proficiency, intended to assist less proficient students and challenge students with higher proficiencies. These are generally included in the Reading/Listening section to help teachers to modify reading/listening activities.

Critical Thinking suggestions focus on a hierarchy of questions using Bloom's taxonomy. These are designed specifically to scaffold questions to move students from knowledge-based questions to higher order thinking.

Vocabulary Expansion builds upon vocabulary introduced in each unit to help students further integrate vocabulary. The expansion activities are offered as word analyses or as vocabulary strategies to reinforce vocabulary skills and provide opportunities for review.

COURSE PLANNERS

Each unit contains approximately eight hours of classroom material, plus expansion, homework, and support material, including MyNorthStarLab. Teachers can customize the units by assigning some exercises for homework and/or eliminating others. To help teachers customize the units for their specific teaching situation, the unit-by-unit teaching suggestions in the *Teacher's Manual* include 1, 2, or 3 stars to indicate the relative importance of each section or exercise as follows:

✪✪✪ **Essential:** Predict, Background and Vocabulary, Listening One, Listen for Main Ideas, Listen for Details, Make Inferences, Express Opinions, Listening Two, Integrate Listenings One and Two, Production

✪✪ **Recommended:** Share Information, Expand, Grammar, Pronunciation, Function

✪ **Optional:** Review, Create, Speaking Topics, Research Topics

Class time available per unit	Sections to complete
8 hours or more	Essential (✪✪✪), Recommended (✪✪), Optional (✪)
6 hours	Essential (✪✪✪), Recommended (✪✪)
4 hours	Essential (✪✪✪) only

For more detailed, downloadable unit-by-unit course planners, visit www.mynorthstarlab.com or www.longman.com/northstar.

ACHIEVEMENT TESTS

The reproducible Achievement Tests allow teachers to evaluate students' progress and to identify areas where students might have problems developing their listening and speaking skills. The Achievement Tests should be given upon completion of the corresponding unit.

Description

There are four parts for every test:

Parts 1 and **2** test students' receptive skills. Part 1 assesses students' mastery of listening comprehension. Part 2 assesses the knowledge of the vocabulary introduced in the unit. **Parts 3** and **4** test students' productive skills. Part 3 assesses students' knowledge of the grammar, pronunciation, and functions introduced in the unit. Part 4 is a speaking test related to the content of the unit.

Administration

All parts of each test should be taken in class and students should not be allowed access to any *NorthStar* materials or to their dictionaries. Students should be able to complete Parts 1–3 within 40 minutes and Part 4 within 10 minutes.

Teachers can decide how to incorporate Part 4 (the speaking task) into their testing situations. Some teachers will assign each speaking task immediately after students complete Parts 1–3; others may decide to set aside another time to complete it.

Scoring the Parts

Parts 1–3: Individual test items are worth one point, for a maximum total of 30 points per test. A student's raw score can be obtained by adding together the number of correct items, or by subtracting the total number of incorrect items from 30. To convert the raw score to a percentage score, multiply it by 3.33.

Part 4: The speaking tasks are evaluated based on speaking skills and function. There are two shorter test items in this part, each worth one point. These should be scored according to the suggestions provided in the answer key for each test. The extended speaking tasks are evaluated holistically using scoring rubrics. The scale ranges from 0–4 and includes information from the listening and fluency/pronunciation, connectedness, structures and vocabulary from the unit, and errors.

Combining scores from Parts 1–3 and Part 4: To get a total Achievement Test score, multiply the extended speaking task score by 2. Add the score for the shorter speaking items to this score for the extended speaking task. Then, add the score in Parts 1–3. Multiply this new score by 2.5 to get a percentage score.

Example 1	Example 2
Score on Test Parts 1–3 = 30	Score on Parts 1–3 = 25
Score on Part 4 (extended task) = 4	Score on Part 4 (extended task) = 2
Multiply 4 × 2	Multiply 2 × 2
Score on Part 4 (shorter items) = 2	Score on Part 4 (shorter items) = 1
Add 10 to 30	Add 5 to 25
Multiply 40 × 2.5	Multiply 30 by 2.5
Total score = 100%	Total score = 72.5%

Using the Scoring Rubrics

The *NorthStar Listening and Speaking* rubrics are adapted from the integrated speaking rubric of TOEFL iBT. Whereas the TOEFL iBT scoring rubric is intended to distinguish levels of English proficiency among candidates to colleges and universities, the *NorthStar* scoring rubrics are intended to show progress in students' speaking at each of the five *NorthStar* levels. Therefore, *NorthStar* scoring bands make finer distinctions than TOEFL iBT's scoring band. In this way, students at each level will be able to both see improvement in their scores and receive high marks. The detailed scoring rubric is included in the Achievement Tests Answer Key.

Relationship between TOEFL iBT Rubric and *NorthStar 1* Integrated Speaking Rubric		
TOEFL iBT		*NorthStar 1*
2		4
1–2		3
1		2
1		1
0		0

OTHER NORTHSTAR COMPONENTS

EXAMVIEW

NorthStar ExamView is a stand-alone CD-ROM that allows teachers to **create and customize** their own *NorthStar* tests.

DVD

The *NorthStar* DVD has **engaging, authentic video clips**, including animation, documentaries, interviews, and biographies, that correspond to the themes in *NorthStar*. Each theme contains a three- to five-minute segment that can be used with either the *Reading and Writing* strand or the *Listening and Speaking* strand. The video clips can also be viewed in MyNorthStarLab.

COMPANION WEBSITE

The companion website, www.longman.com/northstar, includes resources for teachers, such as the scope and sequence, correlations to other Longman products and to state standards, and podcasts from the *NorthStar* authors and series editors.

UNIT 1 Faraway Friends

OVERVIEW

Theme: Friendship

This unit deals with traveling and living in another country. Students examine the concept of making friends all over the world as a way to create world peace.

Listening One: *Hello. This is the Friendship Force* is a telephone conversation, in which a teenage girl inquires into traveling abroad with an organization called the Friendship Force.

Listening Two: *The Best Summer of My Life!* is an interview with a high school student about her experience of spending a summer in Costa Rica.

Critical Thinking

Interpret a photograph
Infer word meaning from context
Differentiate between main ideas and details

Relate the listenings to personal opinions and experiences
Classify information

Listening

Predict content
Identify main ideas
Listen for details
Infer information not explicit in the listening

Listen to an interview
Organize and synthesize information from the listenings
Listen for rhythm in sentences

Speaking

Share experiences
Express opinions
Interview classmates

Practice the correct rhythm of sentences
Ask for more information
Practice introductions

Vocabulary

Use context clues to find meaning
Define words
Use adjectives

Grammar

Present and past tense of *be*

Pronunciation

Rhythm

 MyNorthStarLab
Readiness Check, Background and Vocabulary, Listenings One and Two, Notetaking and Academic Skills Practice, Vocabulary and Grammar, Achievement Test

 NorthStar: Reading and Writing 1
Unit 1 focuses on social networking sites as a way for people to connect with others around the world.

Go to www.mynorthstarlab.com for the MyNorthStarLab *Readiness Check*.

FOCUS ON THE TOPIC

◖ SKILLS

Interpret a photograph; predict content; use prior knowledge; infer the meaning of new vocabulary from context.

✦✦✦ Ⓐ PREDICT

Suggested Time: 5 minutes

1. Read the title of the unit with the class. Elicit ideas from students about the meaning of the title. Ask students to predict what the unit will be about based on the title. Affirm each prediction as a possibility.

2. Discuss question 2 as a class. Elicit ideas from students. Ask follow-up questions such as: *How do you know if the people in the picture are friends or family? What do you see in the picture to give you the answer?*

3. Discuss question 3 with students. Encourage students to share their experiences with the class.

✦✦ Ⓑ SHARE INFORMATION

Suggested Time: 20 minutes

1. Go over the chart in **Exercise 1**. Be sure students understand the questions and the meaning of *host family*. Then have students fill in the first column about themselves.

2. Have students work in pairs to interview each other and fill out the chart.

3. Have students compare their answers and then have pairs present information about each other to the class.

Expansion/Homework
Have students bring in one picture from a travel experience they had. Have students share the picture and experience with the class.

📁 Go to www.mynorthstarlab.com for *Background and Vocabulary.*

Suggested Time: 25 minutes

1. Explain that students will learn about an organization called the Friendship Force. Have students predict what kind of organization it might be. Explain that *force* means *strength, power,* or *energy.* Elicit ideas from students about what *force* in the context of the Friendship Force might mean. If students can't answer, explain that *force* in this context means a group of people from all over the world who become friends.

2. Go over the instructions for **Exercise 1**. Then ask students to look at the list of the Friendship Force countries. Ask students if their country is listed.

3. Have students listen to the radio commercial in **Exercise 2** as they read the text. Encourage them to write any unfamiliar vocabulary or questions about the commercial. Go over students' questions before moving on to the next exercise. Then have students complete **Exercise 3** and share their answer with the class.

4. Have students work in pairs to complete **Exercise 4**. Then go over the answers with the class.

📁 Go to www.mynorthstarlab.com for additional *Background and Vocabulary* practice.

②FOCUS ON LISTENING

◖ SKILLS

Predict content; identify main ideas; listen for details; make inferences based on the information in the listening; express opinions; listen to an interview.

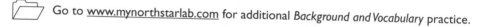

✿✿✿ **A** **LISTENING ONE: Hello. This is the Friendship Force.**

📁 Go to www.mynorthstarlab.com to listen to *Hello. This is the Friendship Force.*

Suggested Time: 5 minutes

Listening One is a telephone conversation between two students about the Friendship Force, an organization that brings people to foreign countries for travel and to live with a host family. The conversational style is somewhat informal.

Have students listen to the beginning of the conversation and answer the questions. Go over the answers and ask students why they chose their answers. Encourage discussion.

✪✪✪ LISTEN FOR MAIN IDEAS   Suggested Time: 10 minutes

1. Have students listen to the complete conversation. Encourage them to take notes. Then have students read the statements in **Exercise 1** and decide whether they are true or false. If necessary, play the interview again to allow students to complete the exercise.

2. Go over the answers with the class. Encourage students to correct the false statements. Next, ask students if their predictions in Section 2A were confirmed. If not, ask them to share what they assumed.

Expansion/Homework

This is a good opportunity to work with students on notetaking strategies. Most students have notetaking strategies they employ in their first language. Elicit a few strategies from the students and introduce some of your own. Encourage students to take notes while listening.

LISTENING STRATEGY: Setting a Purpose for Listening

1. Tell students that, in order to sharpen their listening skills, they need to set a purpose for listening. Explain that they will listen to a telephone conversation to determine if the following statements are true or false.

   • To visit another country you must speak the language.

   • If you have questions about an organization, you have to make an appointment to meet with someone.

   • People, not places, are the most important.

2. Play the audio a second time if necessary. Discuss each statement and have students explain their answers.

✪✪✪ LISTEN FOR DETAILS   Suggested Time: 15 minutes

1. Elicit the difference between main ideas and details. Explain that details support main ideas of a listening. For example, a main idea is that students travel in groups; a detail might be the number of students in each group.

2. Have students listen to the interview again. Then divide the class into small groups and have students complete the exercise.

3. Go over the answers with the whole class. Ask individual students to read the details they completed. If there is disagreement about a detail, listen again to resolve it.

Expansion/Homework

If you have students take notes while listening, ask them to try and complete both exercises using their notes alone. Then allow students to listen again to check their answers and/or fill in any gaps in the exercises.

REACHING ALL STUDENTS: Listen for Details

• **Less Proficient:** Stop the recording at pre-selected intervals for students to record "who" and "what" the section was about.	• **More Proficient:** Stop the recording at pre-selected intervals for students to record the main idea of the section in a complete sentence. Use these topic sentences to tell a summary of the selection.

✪✪✪ MAKE INFERENCES   Suggested Time: 15 minutes

1. Explain that in the following exercise students must determine the correct answers based on information from the conversation. Explain that they will not hear specific answers, but must determine the answers based on what the speakers say.

2. Have students complete the exercise and compare answers with a partner's. Then go over the answers as a class. Encourage discussion.

✪✪✪ EXPRESS OPINIONS   Suggested Time: 15 minutes

Tell students that it is now their turn to express their own opinions about the topic of foreign travel and living with a host family. Give students a few minutes to jot down some ideas for each question. Then have students discuss the questions as a whole class.

CRITICAL THINKING

Give students the following questions for discussion in small groups before discussing as a whole class:

1. Who did Nina speak to about the Friendship Force?

Answer: Nina spoke to Rick at the Friendship Force.

2. List a few reasons Nina was interested in the Friendship Force.

She wanted to learn about another country; she wanted to make new friends; she is interested in traveling; she wanted to go to Thailand.

3. What additional questions would you ask of the Friendship Force representative?

Answers will vary, but students should be encouraged to develop a variety of questions.

4. Do you agree or disagree with living with a host family in another country?

Answers will vary, but students should support their answers.

✪✪✪ B LISTENING TWO: The Best Summer of My Life!

📁 Go to www.mynorthstarlab.com to listen to *The Best Summer of My Life!*

Suggested Time: 10 minutes

Listening Two is an interview with a high school student about her experience living abroad with a host family. The purpose of the listening is to hear more information about traveling abroad from a personal perspective.

1. Have students read the introduction, look at the map, and identify Costa Rica. Have them identify where it is located (Central America). Then have students listen to the interview.

2. Have students complete the exercise. Move around the room and help with any difficult vocabulary. If necessary, replay the interview to allow students to finish the task. Then go over the answers with the class. If there is disagreement, replay excerpts from the interview.

✪✪✪ C INTEGRATE LISTENINGS ONE AND TWO

◀ SKILLS

Organize information from the listenings in a chart; synthesize the information in a role play.

STEP 1: Organize   Suggested Time: 10 minutes

1. Point to the chart and explain that students will compare the Friendship Force and the Experiment in International Living. Tell students they will need to check the column if the information is supplied in the listenings.

2. Have students complete the exercise and then check their answers with a partner's. Finally, go over the answers with the class.

STEP 2: Synthesize   Suggested Time: 20 minutes

1. Explain that students are going to create a role play based on the information in the chart they completed in Step 1. Tell students to make the conversation as natural as possible.

2. Divide the class into pairs and give students a few minutes to complete and practice their role plays. Move around the room and provide help where necessary.

3. If times allows, invite a few pairs to present their conversations to the class.

Expansion/Homework
Students can continue the conversation beyond the lines on the page for homework.

Link to *NorthStar: Reading and Writing 1*

If students are using the companion text, have pairs create a role play based on the information in Readings One and Two. One student wants to join one website (the Friendship Page or MySpace), but doesn't know which. Have students role-play a conversation comparing the two websites and offering advice.

Go to www.mynorthstarlab.com for *Notetaking* and *Academic Skills Practice*.

3 FOCUS ON SPEAKING

A VOCABULARY

◖ SKILLS

Review vocabulary from Listenings One and Two; apply vocabulary to a new context—a conversation; expand vocabulary by identifying and describing people's personalities; use new vocabulary creatively to interview and describe people.

✪ REVIEW   Suggested Time: 10 minutes

Go to www.mynorthstarlab.com for *Review*.

1. Go over the vocabulary in the box in **Exercise 1**. Make sure students know the meaning of each word. Then complete the first item as a class.

2. Have students work individually to complete the exercise. When done, have students compare their answers with another student's, then listen to the conversation to check their answers (**Exercise 2**).

3. If time allows, have students practice the conversation with their partner.

✪✪ EXPAND   Suggested Time: 15 minutes

1. Read the instructions for **Exercise 1** with the class. Explain that the phrases given are ways to ask about someone's personality. Adjectives are used to describe a person. Go over the adjectives with the class. Elicit some example sentences from individual students using the adjectives. For example, *Mia is funny. She tells a lot of jokes.*

2. Go over the instructions and the example in **Exercise 2** with the class. Then have students work in pairs to complete the conversation. Have them take turns. Finally, bring the class together and ask individual students to share their conversations.

Expansion/Homework

Have students bring in pictures of family and friends and post them in front of the class. Then have individual students describe the photo they brought in without identifying which one it is. The other students listen and try to identify which photograph is being described.

VOCABULARY EXPANSION: Tell It Again

1. Compile a list of key words or phrases from the listenings. The words should be listed in the order they appear in the book. For example, *speak to someone, Friendship Force, questions, people travel together, country, host family, visitors, travel around the country, application, thank you.*

2. Remind students that the prefix *re-* means again. Tell students that they will work with a partner to retell the conversations. To guide their speaking, they will use the key words or phrases from the list. The listener will confirm that the speaker has used each of the terms. Then have students switch roles.

✪ CREATE   **Suggested Time: 25 minutes**

1. Explain to students that they will interview three students who will describe themselves using descriptive adjectives. Go over the instructions and the chart in **Exercise 1**.

2. First, have students write three descriptive adjectives about themselves in the first box. Then have them mingle and ask three more students to describe themselves. Have them write the name of the student and the three adjectives. Finally, call on individual students to describe one student who is similar and one who is different from them.

3. Go over the instructions and the chart in **Exercise 2**. First, have students complete the information about themselves and then have them interview three more students to complete the activity. Finally, call on individual students to share one fact about themselves, and one about a classmate.

 Go to www.mynorthstarlab.com for additional *Vocabulary* practice.

✪✪ B GRAMMAR: Present and Past Tense of *Be*

 Go to www.mynorthstarlab.com for *Grammar Chart* and *Exercise 2*.

◖ SKILLS

Learn the present and past tense of *be* and complete a conversation with the appropriate tense.

Suggested Time: 20 minutes

1. Go over the excerpts in **Exercise 1** with the class and have students complete the task. Go over the answers with the class.

2. Go over the chart with the class. Ask individual students to read the explanations and the examples. Elicit more examples from students to make sure they understand the difference between the present and past tenses of *be* and know how to create the questions and negative statements.

3. Explain to students that there are two ways to form contractions with *be* + *not* in the present. Point out that contractions are used in speaking and informal writing. Have students read the contractions aloud to make sure they can pronounce them correctly.

4. Have students complete **Exercise 2**. Go over the answers as a class. Pay special attention to contractions. Then have students practice the conversation in pairs and then ask for volunteers to read the conversation for the class.

Expansion/Homework

(**1**) You can assign Exercise 2 for homework and check answers in class. (**2**) For further practice, offer exercises from *Focus on Grammar 1*, 2nd Edition or Azar's *Basic English Grammar*, 3rd Edition. See the Grammar Book References on page 223 of the student book for specific units and chapters.

 Go to www.mynorthstarlab.com for additional *Grammar* practice.

C SPEAKING

◀ SKILLS

Practice rhythm patterns in speech; practice asking for more information; integrate the concepts, vocabulary, grammar, pronunciation, and function from the unit to introduce and describe people.

✪ PRONUNCIATION: Rhythm

Suggested Time: 20 minutes

1. Start a conversation by asking a student, *Where are you from?* As the student responds, repeat his or her answer placing the rhythm on the appropriate syllable. Use the conversation in the opening of the pronunciation section to guide you. Then ask another student, repeating the pattern. Encourage students to incorporate rhythm into the appropriate syllables. Repeat several times around the class.

2. Play the conversation in **Exercise 1**. Have students read along. Draw their attention to the rhythm of the sentence by looking at the words and syllables in capital letters. Then go over the explanations with the class.

3. Explain that there are several patterns of rhythm in sentences. Explain that rhythm helps the listener follow the conversation and also makes the speaker sound more like a native speaker. Go over each rhythm pattern in **Exercise 2**. Play the audio and have students repeat the sentences. As students get more

comfortable, call on individual students to read the sentences for each pattern aloud. This will allow you to verify that students understand the different patterns.

4. Play the conversation in **Exercise 3** and have students repeat. Then have them practice the conversation with a partner.

5. Go over the instructions and the example in **Exercise 4**. Have students work with a partner to complete the exercise. Then call on pairs to read their completed conversation to the class.

Expansion/Homework

Divide the class into small groups. Have groups repeat after you. This may ease students' embarrassment and allow you to hear a few students at a time rather than the whole class while not singling out one student.

✪✪ FUNCTION: Asking for More Information

Suggested Time: 20 minutes

1. Explain to students that there are specific phrases they can use in a conversation to get more information. With books closed, have students list some phrases they know. Write them on the board.

2. Have students open their books. Call on two students to read the conversation to the class. Then go over the phrases in the chart. Have students add those phrases from the board that are not listed in the chart. Point out the use of *that* to refer to something the speaker just said. Give students this example: A: I can tell you about the Friendship Force. B: Yes, I'd like to know more about that. Explain that *that* refers to *the Friendship Force* in speaker A's statement.

3. Go over the instructions and the example in the exercise. Then have students work in pairs to complete the exercise. Move around the room and provide assistance where necessary. When finished, call on a few pairs to read their conversations to the class.

✪✪✪ PRODUCTION: Introduction

Suggested Time: 30–35 minutes

If you wish to assign a different speaking task than the one in this section, see page 22. The alternative topics relate to the theme of the unit, but may not target the same grammar, pronunciation, or function structures taught in the unit.

1. Divide the class into pairs and have them complete Step 1. Encourage students to ask as many questions as they can. This is their opportunity to learn about their classmates. Answers should include vocabulary, grammar, pronunciation and language for describing personalities and travel from the unit.

2. When the students in each pair have interviewed each other, have them find another pair and complete Step 2. Student A will tell the new pair (C and D) about Student B. Students C and D will ask for more information. Student B will answer. Have pairs continue until all four students have introduced each other.

3. If some pairs finish faster than others, have those pairs do Step 2 again with a new pair.

4. Ask for volunteer groups of four to demonstrate their conversation for the class.

Expansion/Homework

You may want to have students write the questions they plan to ask in the production activity at home.

 Link to *NorthStar: Reading and Writing 1*

If students are also using the companion text, have them incorporate the phrases for greeting and saying good-bye from Expand in Unit 1 of the *Reading and Writing* strand.

✪ ALTERNATIVE SPEAKING TOPICS

These topics give students an alternative opportunity to explore and discuss issues related to the unit theme.

✪ RESEARCH TOPICS

Suggested Time: 20–30 minutes in class

1. Have students turn to page 214. Review the instructions for the activity with the class.

2. Have students choose one organization from the list and research it in the library or on the Internet. Emphasize that students' research should include answers to the questions listed in the book. Encourage students to include additional information they find.

3. Have students present their research findings in small groups. Have other students in the group ask additional questions about the organization.

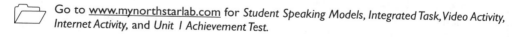 Go to www.mynorthstarlab.com for *Student Speaking Models, Integrated Task, Video Activity, Internet Activity,* and *Unit 1 Achievement Test.*

UNIT 2 Recycled Fashion

OVERVIEW

Theme: Fashion

This unit focuses on the concept of recycling and reusing clothing by a company called Eco-Fashion, and recycling and reusing materials by the women of Gee's Bend, Alabama in quilt making. Students explore and discuss the benefits of reusing and recycling as a benefit to the environment.

Listening One: *Eco-Fashion* is an interview with a designer Deborah Lindquist, in which she describes her eco-fashion line of clothing.

Listening Two: *The Quilts of Gee's Bend* is a radio broadcast about a small town in Alabama, famous for the women who make quilts out of old materials.

Critical Thinking

Interpret pictures
Evaluate trends and preferences
Infer word meaning from context

Differentiate between main ideas and details
Rate and evaluate personal preferences
Classify information

Listening

Predict content
Listen for main ideas
Listen for details
Interpret speakers' tone and attitude
Complete an outline

Organize and synthesize information from the listenings
Listen for word stress
Listen and evaluate student presentations

Speaking

Share opinions
Agree and disagree with statements
Role-play

Practice the correct word stress
Use expressions for checking understanding
Prepare a presentation

Vocabulary

Use context clues to find meaning
Use new words to complete sentences
Use idiomatic expressions

Grammar

Present progressive

Pronunciation

Syllables and word stress

 MyNorthStarLab
Readiness Check, Background and Vocabulary, Listenings One and Two, Notetaking and Academic Skills Practice, Vocabulary and Grammar, Achievement Test

 NorthStar: Reading and Writing 1
Unit 2 focuses on school clothing and whether students should be required to wear uniforms.

Go to www.mynorthstarlab.com for the MyNorthStarLab *Readiness Check*.

1 FOCUS ON THE TOPIC

◀ SKILLS

Interpret a photograph; predict content; use prior knowledge; infer the meaning of new vocabulary from context.

✺✺✺ A PREDICT

Suggested Time: 5 minutes

1. Have students study the picture. Ask them to explain the meaning of the symbol for recycling. Ask them if they have seen this symbol anywhere and if so, where.

2. Discuss the questions as a class. Explain the meaning of *recycle* if students are not familiar with it (to use again for a different purpose). You can ask additional questions such as, *Do students recycle anything? If so, what? What are the benefits of recycling?*

✺✺ B SHARE INFORMATION

Suggested Time: 15 minutes

1. Explain that students will interview each other about where they get their clothes and what they do with old clothing. Have students mingle and interview each other.

2. Tally the number of responses for each item on the board for the whole class. Ask for a show of hands to get the information.

✺✺✺ C BACKGROUND AND VOCABULARY

Go to www.mynorthstarlab.com for *Background and Vocabulary*.

Suggested Time: 20 minutes

1. Explain that students will listen to a radio show where a woman is calling in for advice on what to do with her old clothes. Have students listen to the radio show in **Exercise 1** as they read the text. Encourage them to write any unfamiliar vocabulary or questions they may have about the text. Go over students' questions before moving on to the next exercise.

2. Have students complete **Exercise 2**. Encourage them to underline the places in the text that helped them understand the definitions. Go over the answers as a class.

 Go to www.mynorthstarlab.com for additional *Background and Vocabulary* practice.

#

◀ SKILLS

Predict content; identify main ideas; listen for details; make inferences about speakers' attitudes; express opinions about eco-fashion; listen to a radio broadcast and complete an outline.

 LISTENING ONE: Eco-Fashion

Go to www.mynorthstarlab.com to listen to *Eco-Fashion.*

Suggested Time: 5 minutes

Listening One is an interview with Deborah Lindquist, a fashion designer. She talks about what eco-fashion is and why she designs clothing using old and recycled materials. The conversational style is somewhat informal.

1. Have students read the title of the listening and study the photographs. Ask them what they think eco-fashion is. Write their ideas on the board.

2. Play the excerpt from the interview and have students answer the questions. Call on students to read their answers to the class. Tell them that their answers are predictions and they will listen to the whole interview to see if their predictions are correct.

LISTENING STRATEGY: Listening and Following Directions

Following directions while listening is a very good comprehension practice because it encourages students to focus on the listening selection while following the instructions. Read the instructions for making a paper airplane. Speak slowly and clearly, repeating each line twice. Show a sample of a finished product so students can compare it to their own work. Next, have students write directions for completing a task and read them to others. Remind students to read slowly and clearly, repeating each line twice. Students may be encouraged to research topics to find something to teach the class such as origami, cartoon drawing, or cooking.

How to Make a Paper Airplane

Use a piece of rectangular paper. Fold the paper in half lengthwise and crease.

Open the paper. Fold down the top right corner to the middle crease. Fold down the top left corner to the middle crease. Refold the paper in half lengthwise with the folds inside. Place the paper on a flat surface with the point facing right. Hold paper on the inside fold. To form the right wing, fold one side of the paper down from that point.

To form the left wing, turn the paper over and fold the other side.

✪✪✪ LISTEN FOR MAIN IDEAS
Suggested Time: 10 minutes

1. Have students listen to the interview and complete **Exercise 1**. If necessary, play the interview again to allow students to finish. Then go over the answers as a class.

2. Ask students to return to their predictions and the ideas about eco-fashion on the board. Ask students if their predictions were confirmed. If not, ask students to share what they assumed.

✪✪✪ LISTEN FOR DETAILS
Suggested Time: 15 minutes

1. Elicit the difference between main ideas and details. Explain that details support the main ideas of a listening by giving specific information such as a number or description. For example, a main idea might be that eco-fashion uses old materials. A detail might be specific kinds of materials.

2. Play the interview again and have students complete the exercise.

3. Go over the answers with the whole class. Ask individual students to read the details they completed. If there is disagreement about a detail, listen again to resolve it.

REACHING ALL STUDENTS: Listen for Details

- **Less Proficient:** Have students draw a picture from a detailed description and label it using words or phrases.

- **More Proficient:** Have students create a mind map to represent specific details from the listening. Use the maps to guide an oral summarization.

Expansion/Homework

Give students strategies for taking notes. They can write down individual words, phrases, or sentences. Encourage them to get their ideas on paper without worrying about grammar. Their notes do not need to be complete sentences, just enough to help them recall the information they heard. Encourage them to try and complete both exercises using their notes alone. Then allow students to listen again to check their answers and/or fill in any gaps in the exercises.

✪✪✪ MAKE INFERENCES
Suggested Time: 15 minutes

1. Explain that in the following exercise, students must determine the correct answer based on information from the conversation. Explain that they will not

hear a specific answer, but must determine the answer by using the information they hear.

2. Have students listen to each excerpt, then compare answers with a partner's before going on to the next excerpt. Encourage students to explain why they chose their answer. Give them options—speed of speaking, tone of voice, a specific word. Encourage discussion.

✪✪✪ EXPRESS OPINIONS   Suggested Time: 15 minutes

1. Tell students that it is now their turn to express their own opinions about fashion and the use of old and recycled materials in clothing.

2. Have students complete the activity individually. When done, place students in groups of four to discuss their answers. Have each group assign one recorder, someone to keep track of the responses by tallying the numbers of "agrees" and "disagrees." Encourage students to support their opinions. Emphasize that when expressing an opinion, there is no right answer.

3. When done, ask for the group reporters to report on the group's responses. Encourage students to elaborate on their opinions with the whole class.

CRITICAL THINKING

Give students the following questions for discussion in small groups before discussing as a whole class:

1. What is eco-fashion?

   Answer: Eco-fashion is fashion that uses organic materials.

2. Give two examples of organic materials.

   Answer: Wool and cotton

3. Explain the difference between old material and vintage material.

   Answer: Vintage is one of a kind material from the past.

4. What evidence in the interview suggests people are in favor of recycled clothing?

   Accept any of the following answers: People love wearing unusual and beautiful things. Eco-fashion is becoming trendy. People care about the environment.

✪✪✪ B LISTENING TWO: The Quilts of Gee's Bend

Go to www.mynorthstarlab.com to listen to *The Quilts of Gee's Bend.*

Suggested Time: 15 minutes

Listening Two is a radio broadcast, in which students hear about a group of women in Alabama who make quilts from old clothing and material. The purpose of the listening is to encourage students to think of how materials that have special meaning to people could be preserved in another form—a quilt.

1. Have students read the introduction, look at the map, and identify Alabama. Have students identify where it is located (southern United States). Ask if anyone has ever made a quilt or knows someone who has. Ask if quilts are made in their home countries and if so, describe any tradition around quilt making. Then explain that students will hear a radio broadcast about quilt making in Gee's Bend, Alabama.

2. Have students listen and complete the outline. Go over the answers as a class.

3. If students had commented on traditions around quilts in their countries, take some time to compare and contrast Gee's Bend quilt making.

Expansion/Homework

Do an Internet search for images of quilts from Gee's Band. Bring them to class and have students see if they can identify any of the materials used in the quilts.

✪✪✪ C INTEGRATE LISTENINGS ONE AND TWO

◖ SKILLS

Organize information from the listenings in a chart; synthesize the information in a role play.

STEP 1: Organize
Suggested Time: 10 minutes

1. Point to the chart and explain that students will compare the eco-fashion designer and the women of Gee's Bend by looking at how they are similar or different in what they do and what materials they use.

2. Divide the class into small groups and have students complete the chart. Encourage students to look back at the listening questions and any notes they took. Then go over the answers with the entire class.

STEP 2: Synthesize
Suggested Time: 20 minutes

1. Explain that students are going to role-play an interview based on the information in the chart they completed in Step 1. Tell them that they should make the conversation as natural as possible.

2. Have students work in groups of three. One person is the interviewer, one is the eco-fashion designer, and one is a woman from Gee's Bend. Give groups a few minutes to prepare and practice their interviews. Move around the room and provide help where necessary with pronunciation and vocabulary.

3. When all students are finished, invite a few groups to come up and act out their interviews.

Extension/Homework

(1) Students can continue the conversation beyond the lines on the page for homework. (2) Students can use the Internet to find images of eco-fashion or a Gee's Bend quilt to talk about in their interviews.

Link to *NorthStar: Reading and Writing 1*

If students are using the companion text, have them discuss the letter sent by the school principal to the parents in Reading One. Ask them, *What do you think Deborah Lindquist, the eco-fashion designer, would have to say about school uniforms?*

 Go to www.mynorthstarlab.com for *Notetaking* and *Academic Skills Practice*.

③ FOCUS ON SPEAKING

Ⓐ VOCABULARY

◀ SKILLS

Review vocabulary from Listenings One and Two; apply vocabulary to a new context—a radio advertisement; expand vocabulary by learning and using idioms related to clothing; use new vocabulary creatively in a conversation.

✪ REVIEW   Suggested Time: 10 minutes

 Go to www.mynorthstarlab.com for *Review*.

1. Look at the list of vocabulary items in the box and have students practice pronouncing each one after you. Then have students study the pictures that illustrate the process of fleece making. Explain any unfamiliar vocabulary.

2. Have students complete the exercise. Go over the answers as a class.

✪✪ EXPAND   Suggested Time: 15 minutes

1. Explain that students will learn a group of idioms related to clothing. Explain that idioms are phrases or sentences whose meaning can't be determined from knowing the meaning of the individual words. Give an example they are likely to know *(That test was a piece of cake)*.

2. Read the conversation in **Exercise 1** aloud with a student. Discuss the main idea of the conversation with the class. Ask questions to help them determine the meanings of the idioms. For example, *Does B think A is dressed nicely? Does the dress fit well or not?*

3. Have students repeat after you to practice the list of idioms in **Exercise 2**. Then have students complete the exercise. Go over the answers as a class.

Expansion/Homework
Have students keep a book of idioms and phrases they are learning. They can categorize it by topic or alphabetically. Encourage students to include the idiom, the meaning, and an example sentence.

VOCABULARY EXPANSION: Context Clues

Provide students with the vocabulary list and a copy of the audioscript. Students will locate the target word in the text and record the sentence containing the word. Tell students if the sentence does not help clarify the meaning of the word, they should read other sentences. Assign discussion pairs to share clues that helped determine the meaning of each word.

○ CREATE

Suggested Time: 20 minutes

1. Explain to students that they will have a conversation about recycled clothing. One student is a customer, the other a recycled clothing and quilt store owner.

2. Go over the example with the class. Then have students work in pairs to create their own conversation. Have students use vocabulary from Review and Expand. Allow students to write down ideas they want to include in their conversation, but discourage writing out the whole conversation.

3. Ask for volunteers to share their conversation with the class.

 Go to www.mynorthstarlab.com for additional *Vocabulary* practice.

○○ B GRAMMAR: Present Progressive

 Go to www.mynorthstarlab.com for *Grammar Chart* and *Exercise 4*.

◀ SKILLS

Learn and use the present progressive tense.

Suggested Time: 30 minutes

1. Read the sentences in **Exercise 1** with students, having them repeat after you. Have them underline the verb in each sentence. Then have students answer the questions in **Exercise 2**. Go over the answers with the class. Have students answer the questions in **Exercise 3**. Then explain that the present progressive is used to describe actions that are currently happening. They don't need to be actions you can see, but just occurring now.

2. Go over the chart with the class. Ask individual students to read the example sentences and explanations. Assist students with any pronunciation difficulties by having the whole class repeat after you. Also, ask follow up questions after each explanation and have students underline subjects and verbs.

3. Point out that *yes / no* questions are formed by placing the verb *be* before the subject. Contrast this with *wh-* questions with the *wh-* word in front of the verb *be* and the verb *be* in front of the subject.

4. Point out that negatives are formed by placing *not* between the verb *be* and the main verb. Finally, go over spelling for a consonant/vowel/consonant pattern where the final consonant is doubled when adding *-ing*.

5. Have students complete **Exercise 4**. To check answers, call on a pair of students to read the completed conversation. Correct any errors.

6. Have students work in pairs to complete **Exercise 5**. One student looks at page 36, the other looks at page 207. Students take turns asking and answering questions about the pictures using the present progressive. Students should not show each other their respective pictures. They should find two things that are the same, and two that are different about their pictures. Move around the room helping with pronunciation, vocabulary, and grammar.

Expansion/Homework

For further practice, offer exercises from *Focus on Grammar 1*, 2nd Edition or Azar's *Basic English Grammar*, 3rd Edition. See the Grammar Book References on page 223 of the student book for specific units and chapters.

 Go to www.mynorthstarlab.com for additional *Grammar* practice.

C SPEAKING

◖SKILLS

Practice syllables and stress in words; use words and phrases to check for understanding; integrate the concepts, vocabulary, grammar, pronunciation, and function from the unit in a presentation.

◌◌ PRONUNCIATION: Syllables and Word Stress

Suggested Time: 20 minutes

1. Write the words *woman, designer* and *new* on the board. Have students repeat them after you. Clap out the syllables as they pronounce the words. Explain that you are clapping out the syllables, or parts of the words. Have students tell you how many syllables are in each word. Ask if students hear a difference in loudness for any of the syllables. Explain that the loudness is called word stress.

2. Play the conversation in **Exercise 1** as students read. Have students tell you how many syllables are in each boldfaced word. Then go over the information in the chart and have students repeat the words after you.

3. Play the words in **Exercise 2** and have students repeat the words and then underline the syllables. Students should write a line over the stressed syllables then repeat again making sure the stressed syllables are long. Go over the answers with the class.

4. Play the sentences in **Exercise 3a** and have students repeat them and then underline the stressed syllables. Then divide the class into pairs and have students complete **Exercise 3b**. Call on pairs to share their answers with the class.

5. Play the conversation for **Exercise 4**. Have students fill in the blanks. You will most likely have to play the audio several times. Have students compare their answers after each time you play. Play it two to three times and then go over the answers as a class. Finally, have pairs practice the conversation.

Expansion/Homework
Encourage students to mark syllables and stress as they learn new words. This will help them remember how to pronounce the words.

✪✪ FUNCTION: Checking for Understanding

Suggested Time: 20 minutes

1. Explain to students that as we speak, we commonly check that the listener understands what we are saying. With books closed, have students list some phrases for checking understanding they know. Write them on the board.

2. Read the instructor's explanation in **Exercise 1** with a student. Then go over the phrases in the box. Have students repeat after you. Help with pronunciation as needed. Finally, have students add those phrases from the board that are not listed in the chart.

3. Have students work in groups of four to complete **Exercise 2**. Each student chooses one of the choices. Students take turns explaining how to do the activity. Students should use the expressions to check for understanding. Other students in the group should respond appropriately and ask questions. Move around the room and help with vocabulary.

Expansion/Homework
(1) For students who finish the task quickly, have them rotate choices and choose another task to explain. (2) Students can choose an activity they are very familiar with and describe it to the class. Being familiar with an activity can give them a sense of confidence in completing it.

✪✪✪ PRODUCTION: Presentation

Suggested Time: 45–50 minutes

If you wish to assign a different speaking task than the one in this section, see page 42. The alternative topics relate to the theme of the unit, but may not target the same grammar, pronunciation, or function taught in the unit.

1. Divide the class into pairs. Explain that students will now have an opportunity to create something new from old materials. They will decide what it is and what it is made of.

2. Have pairs begin by choosing two or more of the materials from the list in Step 1. They can use other materials they know. Once they have chosen materials, have students discuss how these materials can be used and then draw

the object (Steps 2 and 3). The picture does not need to be a perfect representation, just enough so they can explain it to the class.

3. Have pairs discuss what they will make and how they will make it. Write the following questions on the board to guide their discussions and presentations: *What is the object? What is it made of? How can it be used? What is the step-by-step process in making it? Describe it.* Students should use vocabulary and grammar from the unit as well as phrases to check for understanding.

4. In Step 4, have pairs take turns presenting their new clothing or object to the class. Students in the class will listen to the presentation and ask questions.

 Link to *NorthStar: Reading and Writing 1*
If students are also using the companion text, have them incorporate the phrases from Expand in Unit 2 of the *Reading and Writing* strand.

✪ ALTERNATIVE SPEAKING TOPICS

These topics give students an alternative opportunity to explore and discuss issues related to the unit theme.

✪ RESEARCH TOPICS

Suggested Time: 20–30 minutes in class

1. Have students turn to page 215. Review the instructions for the activity with the class.

2. Have students interview a person using the questions listed and then write a short report summarizing their findings. Encourage them to use additional questions.

3. Have students present their reports in small groups. Have other students in the group ask additional questions.

 Go to www.mynorthstarlab.com for *Student Speaking Models, Integrated Task, Video Activity, Internet Activity,* and *Unit 2 Achievement Test.*

Rap Music

OVERVIEW

Theme: The arts
  This unit focuses on the topic of rap music. Students learn the history of rap and discuss the pros and cons of this type of music.

Listening One: *A Famous Rapper: Tupac Shakur* is an interview between a DJ and a famous rapper, King Kool discussing the history and origins of rap.

Listening Two: *Rap—Good or Bad?* is a conversation between a music producer, a professor of education, and the members of the Parents' Organization, discussing the pros and cons of rap.

Critical Thinking

Analyze and label a picture
Activate prior knowledge
Relate listenings to personal values
Infer information not explicit in the listening

Infer word meaning from context
Evaluate negative and positive aspects of rap music
Classify information
Express likes and dislikes

Listening

Predict content
Listen for main ideas and correct false statements
Listen for details
Infer speakers' opinions and attitudes

Identify opinions
Organize and synthesize information from the listenings
Classify sounds
Listen to student interviews

Speaking

Ask and answer questions
Express opinions about rap music
Share personal opinions and knowledge about music

Role-play
Practice pronouncing vowel sounds
Use appropriate language for expressing opinions
Conduct an interview

Vocabulary

Use context clues to find meaning
Define words
Classify expressions of like and dislike

Grammar

Simple present tense with non-action (stative) verbs

Pronunciation

/ɪ/ and /iy/

 MyNorthStarLab
Readiness Check, Background and Vocabulary, Listenings One and Two, Notetaking and Academic Skills Practice, Vocabulary and Grammar, Achievement Test

 NorthStar: Reading and Writing 1
Unit 3 focuses on the life and work of Keith Haring.

Go to www.mynorthstarlab.com for the MyNorthStarLab *Readiness Check*.

FOCUS ON THE TOPIC

◖ SKILLS

Label a photograph; predict content; use prior knowledge; infer the meaning of new vocabulary from context.

✪✪✪ A PREDICT

Suggested Time: 10 minutes

1. Look at the title of the unit. Ask students if they know what rap is and if they listen to it. Then look at the picture and have students describe what they see. Let them call out vocabulary. After a few minutes, complete **Exercise 1** as a class. Then spend a few minutes pronouncing the words and having students repeat after you.

2. Have students answer the questions in **Exercise 2**. Explain that they will learn the answers later in the unit.

✪✪ B SHARE INFORMATION

Suggested Time: 20 minutes

1. Ask students to name some musicians or bands they like. Ask students to say one or two sentences about the band (kind of music, where they are from, etc.).

2. Have students look at the pictures. Ask if anyone is familiar with the musicians or groups in the pictures. Go over pronunciation of the names.

3. Have students move around the class, ask the questions, and complete **Exercise 1**. Have students write down the answers. Then bring the class back together and ask for volunteers to answer the questions in **Exercise 2**.

✪✪✪ C BACKGROUND AND VOCABULARY

Go to www.mynorthstarlab.com for *Background and Vocabulary*.

Suggested Time: 25 minutes

1. Explain that students will listen to a conversation between two college roommates. Have students read as they listen to the conversation in **Exercise 1** and pay attention to the boldfaced words. If other words or phrases are

unfamiliar, have students underline them. Go over students' questions before they complete the next exercise.

2. Have students work in pairs to complete **Exercise 2**. Encourage them to point to the place in the text where the answers can be found. When done, go over the answers as a class.

3. Have students complete **Exercise 3**. Start by going over pronunciation of the words in the box. As you pronounce the words, write them on the board. Have students mark out syllables and stress of each word as you mark them on the board. Go over the answers as a class.

 Go to www.mynorthstarlab.com for additional *Background and Vocabulary* practice.

②FOCUS ON LISTENING

◖SKILLS

Predict content; identify main ideas; listen for details; make inferences; express opinions; listen to a conversation and identify opinions.

✪✪✪Ⓐ LISTENING ONE: A Famous Rapper: Tupac Shakur

 Go to www.mynorthstarlab.com to listen to *A Famous Rapper: Tupac Shakur.*

Suggested Time: 5 minutes

Listening One is a radio interview with rapper King Kool about the history of rap and a famous rapper, Tupac Shakur. The conversational style is informal.

1. Have students listen to the beginning of the conversation and answer the questions. Encourage students to take notes.

2. Go over the answers as a class. Explain to students that their answers are just predictions and they will find out if they were correct after listening to the whole interview.

LISTENING STRATEGY: Listening Guides

1. In order to set a purpose for listening, provide students with a framework or guide. Tell students that a guide for listening can help them focus on the task. As a whole group, develop questions to use in a guide. For example, *What do I know about the topic? What do I expect to find out? Who is the speaker? What is the main idea of the interview? What information is presented about the topic?*

2. Following the audio, allow time for students to discuss and demonstrate an understanding of the material. Extend the lesson by assigning students the task of writing an informative paragraph on the topic using the newly acquired information.

REACHING ALL STUDENTS: Listening Guides

- **Less Proficient:** Have students listen to small sections of the audio, pausing to record their responses to the guide questions.

- **More Proficient:** Have students record their responses to the guide questions as they listen to the audio. Replay the recording and allow students to confirm or extend their answers.

✪✪✪ LISTEN FOR MAIN IDEAS
Suggested Time: 15 minutes

1. Have students listen to the complete interview and then complete **Exercise 1**. Remind them that they need to correct the false statements. Then go over the answers as a class.

2. Ask students if their predictions in Section 2A, Question 3 were correct. If not, ask students to share what they assumed.

✪✪✪ LISTEN FOR DETAILS
Suggested Time: 10 minutes

1. Elicit the difference between main ideas and details. Explain that details support the main ideas of a listening by giving specific information. For example, a main idea might be that rap music started a long time ago. A detail might be the date when it started (1970s).

2. Play the interview again and have students complete the exercise.

3. Go over the answers with the whole class. Ask individual students to read the details they completed. If there is disagreement about a detail, listen again to resolve it.

Expansion/Homework
Give students strategies for taking notes. They can write down individual words, phrases, or sentences. Encourage them to get their ideas on paper without worrying about grammar. Their notes do not need to be complete sentences, just enough to help them recall the information they heard. Encourage them to try and complete both exercises using their notes alone. Then allow students to listen again to check their answers and/or fill in any gaps in the exercises.

✪✪✪ MAKE INFERENCES
Suggested Time: 15 minutes

1. Explain that in the following exercise students must determine the correct answers based on information from the interview. Explain that they will not hear the specific answers, but must determine the answers by inferring the information.

2. Have students listen to each excerpt, circle the answer, and then compare answers with a partner's before going on to the next excerpt. Ask students to

explain why they chose their answer. Encourage discussion. Then go over the answers as a class.

✪✪✪ EXPRESS OPINIONS

Suggested Time: 15 minutes

1. Tell students that it is now their turn to express their own opinions about the topic of rap music.

2. Divide the class into small groups. In each group, one student will take notes on the responses. The notes do not need to be complete sentences, just ideas. Another student will report to the class. Have groups decide who will do these roles.

3. Have the groups discuss the questions. When done, ask for the group reporters to report on their group's responses.

CRITICAL THINKING

Give students the following questions for discussion in small groups before discussing as a whole class:

1. According to King Kool, how did rap music change in the 80s?

   Answer: King Kool thinks 80s rap songs have meaning because rappers wrote about their lives.

2. Who is King Kool?

   Answer: King Kool was one of the first rappers in the 70s.

3. What information supports the statement, "I'm going to die young?"

   Answer: Tupac was only 25 when he died.

4. Do you agree or disagree that rap music is about anger?

   Answers will vary, but students should support their answers with reasons.

Expansion/Homework

Have students bring in CDs of their favorite musician or band. Let students play a song and tell the class about the musician/band.

✪✪✪ B LISTENING TWO: Rap—Good or Bad?

📁 Go to www.mynorthstarlab.com to listen to *Rap—Good or Bad?*

Suggested Time: 15 minutes

Listening Two is an excerpt from a Parents' Organization meeting. Students hear opposing views on rap music as presented by Robbie Simon, a music producer and Brad Crosby, a professor of education.

1. Ask students why they think people might not like rap. Write some examples on the board. Ask if they think young people have different opinions of rap than older people. If so, why?

2. Explain that students will hear a conversation between a music producer, an educator, and members of a Parents' Organization about rap.

3. Have students listen to the conversation and complete the exercise. When done, go over the answers as a class.

4. If time permits, take a poll to see how many students agree with Mr. Simon, Professor Crosby, the principal, and the parents.

✪✪✪ C INTEGRATE LISTENINGS ONE AND TWO

◀ SKILLS

Organize information from the listenings in a chart; synthesize the information in a role play.

STEP 1: Organize   Suggested Time: 10 minutes

1. Point to the chart and explain that students will list the good and bad things about rap. In the chart, they will see incomplete sentences. Working in pairs, have students complete the sentences.

2. Go over the answers with the class.

STEP 2: Synthesize   Suggested Time: 20 minutes

1. Have students continue to work in pairs. Explain that they are going to create a role play based on the information in the chart they completed in Step 1. Tell students that they should make the conversation as natural as possible and to use all three reasons listed in Step 1.

2. Give students a few minutes to prepare and practice their conversations. Move around the room and provide help where necessary with pronunciation and vocabulary.

3. If time allows, invite a few pairs to come up and act out their conversations.

Extension/Homework

You might want to have students use the Internet to learn more about the pros and cons of rap then continue the conversation for homework.

Link to *NorthStar: Reading and Writing 1*

If students are also using the companion text, have them discuss what Keith Haring would say about rap music. How would he say his art and rap are alike?

 Go to www.mynorthstarlab.com for *Notetaking* and *Academic Skills Practice*.

3 FOCUS ON SPEAKING

A VOCABULARY

◖ SKILLS

Review vocabulary from Listenings One and Two; apply vocabulary to a new context—a conversation; expand vocabulary by learning and using expressions for likes and dislikes; use new vocabulary creatively in a conversation.

✪ REVIEW

Suggested Time: 15 minutes

1. Have students work in pairs. Explain that each student will see a part of the conversation. Student A looks at page 53, Student B looks at pages 208–209.

2. Explain that Student A starts by asking question 1. Have Students A repeat the question after you. Then, as Students B look at pages 208–209, point out the title of their conversation (*I don't like rap.*) and have them pick the appropriate response (*No, I don't think rap is real music.*). Then Students A make the next comment. Have Students B respond. Once you are sure students understand the activity, have the pairs start over to complete the conversation, then continue with Conversation 2.

✪✪ EXPAND

Suggested Time: 15 minutes

 Go to www.mynorthstarlab.com for *Expand*.

1. Draw a vertical line on the board. Label the top of the line 5, and the bottom 0. Explain that this is a rating scale with 0 meaning "bad feelings" and 5 meaning "good feelings." Explain that a scale is a way to measure something. Give some examples of scales (a bathroom scale, a thermometer, etc.).

2. Look at the example in **Exercise 1** with students. Explain that *I love it* is a way to show you really like something and have good feelings about it. Have students read the phrases in the box and find another phrase that shows strong feelings of like (*I like it a lot.*). Have students write it on the line.

3. Have students look at a phrase that indicates not liking something at all (*I hate it*). Explain that they will rank the rest of the phrases based on how much or how little it indicates liking.

4. Have students work in pairs to complete the scale. When done, go over the answers with the whole class by completing the scale on the board (**Exercise 2**). Then have students practice repeating the phrases after you.

5. Have students mingle and ask two other students the questions in **Exercise 3**. Have students take notes on the responses. Then bring the class back together and ask for volunteers to share the responses.

✪ CREATE

Suggested Time: 20 minutes

1. Have students work in small groups. Each student will ask one question, and take notes on the responses.

2. Have students take turns asking their questions to each member of the group. Encourage students to use vocabulary from Review and phrases from Expand.

3. Bring the class back together and ask for volunteers to share responses.

 Go to www.mynorthstarlab.com for additional *Vocabulary* practice.

✪✪ B GRAMMAR: Simple Present Tense with Non-Action (Stative) Verbs

 Go to www.mynorthstarlab.com for *Grammar Chart* and *Exercise 3*.

◖ SKILLS

Learn the simple present tense with non-action (stative) verbs and complete a conversation.

Suggested Time: 25 minutes

1. Ask students to name some verbs. Write them on the board. Make two columns as you write them; one with action verbs and one with non-action verbs. When you have a good list, ask students if they know what is different about the two lists. If they can't answer, point to an action verb and ask a student to act it out. Repeat two or three times, pointing out that the student is showing an action. Then point to a verb in the non-action list and ask for a student to act it out. Explain that some verbs are called stative, or non-action verbs. These verbs describe situations, ideas, feelings, and senses.

2. Read the sentences in **Exercise 1** with students. Then have students underline the verbs. Ask them which verbs are non-action verbs. Have students circle them.

3. Go over the chart with the class. Ask individual students to read the explanations and the examples. Assist students with any pronunciation difficulties by having the whole class repeat after you. This way no student is singled out as having difficulty pronouncing a word.

4. Emphasize that some verbs are not used with the present progressive (for example, *know*). Point out that some verbs have two meanings, such as *think*. Finally, go over the list of verbs that have both non-action and action meanings. Encourage students to keep a list, so they can remember these verbs.

5. Have students complete **Exercise 2**. When done, have them compare answers with a partner's and discuss any answers they disagree on. Then go over the answers as a class.

6. Have students complete the conversation in **Exercise 3** individually. Remind them that stative verbs do not use *-ing*. When done, go over the answers as a class. Then have students practice the conversation in pairs.

Expansion/Homework

For further practice, offer exercises from *Focus on Grammar 1*, 2nd Edition or Azar's *Basic English Grammar*, 3rd Edition. See the Grammar Book References on page 223 of the student book for specific units and chapters.

 Go to www.mynorthstarlab.com for additional *Grammar* practice.

Ⓒ SPEAKING

◖ SKILLS

Practice /ɪ/ versus /iy/; learn and practice phrases to express opinions; integrate the concepts, vocabulary, grammar, pronunciation, and function from the unit to conduct student interviews.

◐◑ PRONUNCIATION: /ɪ/ vs. /iy/

Suggested Time: 20 minutes

1. Look at the pictures showing the mouth. Write the two sounds, /iy/ and /ɪ/, on the board. Show students how each sound is produced using example words (*believe, think*). Go over the explanations in the chart.

2. Explain that students will hear pairs of words, one for each sound. Have students listen to the words in **Exercise 1** and circle the ones they hear. Go over the answers as a class. Then read each word and have students repeat after you.

3. Have students listen to the words in **Exercise 2** and repeat them. Then have them circle the words they hear. Go over the answers as a class.

4. Have students work in pairs to complete **Exercise 3**. This exercise will give students valuable feedback as to their pronunciation. Encourage students to write the word they hear, not what they think their partner is saying.

5. Play the conversation in **Exercise 4** for the class and have students repeat. Then have students work in groups of three to practice the conversation. Walk around the room and provide assistance as necessary.

Expansion/Homework

If students need more practice discriminating the sounds, read randomly from the lists and have students raise their right hand if they hear /iy/ and their left hand if they hear /ɪ/. Continue this until the class is able to discriminate the sounds.

⊙⊙ FUNCTION: Expressing Opinions

Suggested Time: 30 minutes

1. Explain to students that there are specific phrases they can use in a conversation when expressing an opinion. Ask if students know other phrases they can use to show they are expressing their opinions. Write them on the board.

2. Go over the phrases in the box. Have students repeat after you. Help with pronunciation as needed. Then have students add those phrases from the board that are not listed in the box.

3. Have students work in groups of three or four. Once in their groups, have one student read the introduction in **Exercise 1** aloud. Once each group has read the introduction, explain that the groups will read a set of statements and then each student will express an opinion on the statement. Students should take turns reading the statements aloud for their group and then go around until each student has expressed an opinion. Have groups complete **Exercise 2**.

4. When done, bring the class back together. Read each statement and ask for one or two volunteers to express an opinion.

⊙⊙⊙ PRODUCTION: Student Interviews

Suggested Time: 40–45 minutes

If you wish to assign a different speaking task than the one in this section, see page 63. The alternative topics relate to the theme of the unit, but may not target the same grammar, pronunciation, or function taught in the unit.

1. Tell students that they will now have an opportunity to interview classmates about music likes and dislikes. Go over the information in the task box with the class.

2. Start with Step 1, asking students to brainstorm different types of music as you write them on the board. Ideas might include, rock, pop, classical, jazz, reggae, rap, techno, opera. Then have students look at the list and choose two kinds of music they like and two kinds they dislike. Ask students to suggest some reasons they like or dislike that style of music. Write some suggestions on the board (*It's boring. It's too slow. It's too loud. It's very interesting.*).

3. In Step 2, have students divide a sheet of paper into two columns, then three rows. They should now have a paper divided into six boxes. Tell students to walk around the classroom, interview six classmates, and write responses in each box (Step 3). Encourage students to use grammar and vocabulary from the unit.

4. When done, have each student report on one student they interviewed. Don't allow students to report on the same student. This will ensure they are listening to their classmates so they do not repeat the answers.

 Link to NorthStar: Reading and Writing 1
If students are also using the companion text, have them complete a similar peer interview activity about artists they know and like or dislike.

✪ ALTERNATIVE SPEAKING TOPICS

These topics give students an alternative opportunity to explore and discuss issues related to the unit theme.

✪ RESEARCH TOPICS

Suggested Time: 20–30 minutes in class

1. Have students turn to pages 215–216. Review the instructions for the activity with the class.

2. Have students complete the task at home and prepare a report. In class, have students play the song and present their reports. Encourage other students to ask additional questions.

 Go to www.mynorthstarlab.com for *Student Speaking Models, Integrated Task, Video Activity, Internet Activity,* and *Unit 3 Achievement Test.*

UNIT 4 Something Valuable

Theme: Special possessions
This unit focuses on the topic of valuable possessions, specifically diamonds. Students explore the topic and learn what makes diamonds so valuable. They also discuss things that hold special value to them.

Listening One: *The Hope Diamond* is an excerpt from a museum tour, in which a tour guide explains the history of the Hope Diamond.

Listening Two: *The Four Cs* is a radio advertisement for a store that sells diamonds.

Critical Thinking

Interpret a photograph
Categorize information
Infer word meaning from context
Infer information not explicit in the listening

Hypothesize another's point of view
Support opinions with reasons
Problem solve
Reach a consensus

Listening

Predict content
Place main ideas in sequential order
Listen for supporting details
Infer speakers' feelings and attitudes

Listen to an advertisement
Organize and synthesize information from the
    listenings
Listen to role plays

Speaking

Share opinions and experiences
Ask and answer questions
Agree and disagree with statements

Make suggestions
Role-play a conversation

Vocabulary

Use context clues to find meaning
Use new vocabulary to complete a conversation
Use idiomatic expressions

Grammar

The simple present

Pronunciation

-S endings for present tense

MyNorthStarLab
Readiness Check, Background and
Vocabulary, Listenings One and Two,
Notetaking and Academic Skills Practice,
Vocabulary and Grammar, Achievement Test

NorthStar: Reading and Writing 1
Unit 4 focuses on collecting valuable or
special possessions.

FOCUS ON THE TOPIC

◖SKILLS

Label a photograph; predict content; use prior knowledge; infer the meaning of new vocabulary from context.

✿✿✿ A PREDICT

Suggested Time: 10 minutes

1. Have students look at the picture and identify any vocabulary they know. Label the items as a class and go over pronunciation of the words.

2. Ask the class if any of the items have a special meaning. If so, what. If not, ask where they have seen the items used or worn. Finally, ask if anyone in the class has a special piece of jewelry they are wearing. If so, have them offer a brief explanation of what the jewelry is and whether it has a special meaning.

✿✿ B SHARE INFORMATION

Suggested Time: 20 minutes

1. Divide the class into groups of three. Have students write the names of each student in the group, starting with their own name. Then have students complete the first column for themselves silently.

2. When done, have students in the group take turns answering the questions. Have them complete the information in the chart.

3. Call on individual students to report their findings to the class.

Expansion/Homework

If you have many students in class who are from different countries, have a follow up discussion on their feelings about wearing jewelry that is popular in their country. Do they notice a difference on gender lines between their country and this one? Does it affect whether they wear their jewelry or not?

 Go to www.mynorthstarlab.com for *Background and Vocabulary*.

Suggested Time: 20 minutes

1. Ask the class if anyone knows anything about the history of diamonds. Ask them to share any information with the class.

2. Explain that students will read and listen to a history of diamonds. Encourage them to underline any unfamiliar words as they read along while listening.

3. When done, ask simple comprehension questions such as: *When were diamonds first collected? When were they first used as engagement rings? Where are they from? Who is DeBeers?*

4. Have students work in pairs to complete the matching exercise. When done, go over the answers as a class.

Go to www.mynorthstarlab.com for additional *Background and Vocabulary* practice.

②FOCUS ON LISTENING

◖SKILLS

Predict content; identify main ideas; listen for details; make inferences; express opinions about diamonds; listen to an advertisement.

✸✸✸ **A** **LISTENING ONE: The Hope Diamond**

Go to www.mynorthstarlab.com to listen to *The Hope Diamond*.

Suggested Time: 5 minutes

Listening One is an excerpt from a museum tour. Students learn about the origin and history of the Hope Diamond. The conversational style is somewhat informal.

1. Have students look at the picture and describe what they see. Ask them if they think the object is valuable and why. Ask what they think the title means.

2. Have students listen to the beginning of the conversation and answer the questions. Ask students to share their answers and say why they chose them.

✸✸✸ LISTEN FOR MAIN IDEAS   **Suggested Time: 10 minutes**

1. Have students listen to the complete conversation. Have them complete **Exercise 1** individually and compare their answers with a partner's.

2. Go over the answers as a class. If there is any disagreement, listen to the conversation again, stopping where appropriate to resolve it.

3. Ask students if their predictions from Section 2A were correct. If not, ask students to share what they assumed.

LISTENING STRATEGY: Getting the Idea

Tell students that they don't have to understand every word to get the general idea. To illustrate, play the first section of the audio and have students freewrite or draw the idea they get from the piece. Then play the piece again and ask students to listen for specific details they can add to their sentences(s) or drawings. Have students compare their work with a partner's before returning to the whole group for discussion.

✪✪✪ LISTEN FOR DETAILS

Suggested Time: 15 minutes

1. Elicit the difference between main ideas and details. Explain that details support the main ideas of a listening by giving specific information such as a number or description. For example, a main idea might be that the Hope Diamond is valuable. A detail might be that it is worth $250 million.

2. Play the recording again and have students complete the exercise. Then go over the answers with the whole class. Ask individual students to read the details they completed. If there is disagreement about a detail, listen again to resolve it.

Expansion/Homework

Ask your students to take notes in an outline while listening. Ask them to try and complete Listen for Details from their notes alone. Then allow students to listen again to check their answers and/or fill in any gaps in the exercise.

✪✪✪ MAKE INFERENCES

Suggested Time: 10 minutes

1. Explain that in the following exercise students must determine the correct answers based on information from the conversation. Explain that they will not hear specific answers, but must determine the answers based on what the speakers say.

2. Have students listen to each excerpt, circle the answer, and then compare answers with a partner's before going on to the next excerpt. Encourage students to explain why they chose their answer. Encourage discussion.

3. Go over the answers as a class.

REACHING ALL STUDENTS: Make Inferences

- **Less Proficient:** Perform pantomimes of simple actions. Ask students to infer from the actions what is taking place in the scenes. For example, *Read a book. Talk on the phone.*

- **More Proficient:** Have students perform pantomimes of advanced actions. Other group members infer from the actions what is taking place in the scenes. For example, *Look at your watch, tap your foot,* and *look in the distance.*

✪✪✪ EXPRESS OPINIONS   Suggested Time: 15 minutes

1. Tell students that it is now their turn to express their own opinions about diamonds.

2. Divide the class into small groups. Have students complete the activity individually and discuss their answers in the group. Students should explain their answers.

3. When done, bring the class together. Take a class poll and write the results on the board for each statement. Encourage a class discussion.

CRITICAL THINKING

Give students the following questions for discussion in small groups before discussing as a whole class:

1. What was the purpose of the tour?

   Answer: The purpose of the tour was to see the Hope Diamond.

2. Why is it called the "Blue Diamond of the Crown?"

   Answer: The diamond became know as the "Blue Diamond of the Crown" because it was a blue diamond owned by King Louis XIV.

3. After the diamond was stolen, where did it reappear?

   Answer: The diamond reappeared in London.

4. What would you have done if you were the American woman who bought the diamond?

   Answers will vary.

📁 Go to www.mynorthstarlab.com to listen to *The Four Cs*.

Suggested Time: 10 minutes

Listening Two is a radio advertisement in which students hear how one company advertises diamonds. The listening gives students the opportunity to learn what qualities make a valuable diamond.

1. Ask students what they think makes a good diamond. Brainstorm ideas (size, shape, color, clarity). Encourage students to explain why they think these qualities make a diamond more valuable.

2. Have students listen to the radio advertisement in **Exercise 1** and then complete **Exercise 2**.

3. When done, have students compare answers with a partner's. Ask for a show of hands if pairs have different answers. If so, play the advertisement again to check the answers.

✿✿✿ **C** **INTEGRATE LISTENINGS ONE AND TWO**

◀ **SKILLS**

Organize information from the listenings in a chart; synthesize the information in a role play.

STEP 1: Organize   **Suggested Time: 15 minutes**

1. Point to the chart and explain that students will consider the Four Cs they learned about in Listening Two and how they relate to the Hope Diamond and diamonds in general.

2. Divide the class into small groups and have students complete the exercise by checking which of the Four Cs applies to each question. Tell students that they need to support their answers with information from the listenings.

3. Go over the answers with the class.

STEP 2: Synthesize   **Suggested Time: 20 minutes**

1. Explain that students are going to create a role play based on the information in the chart they completed in Step 1. Tell students that they should make the conversations as natural as possible.

2. Have students work in pairs. Student A is a diamond salesperson, Student B wants to purchase a pair of diamond earrings. Have students complete the role play using the information from the chart in Step 1. When done, students should switch roles. Move around the room and provide help where necessary with pronunciation and vocabulary.

3. If time allows, invite a few pairs to come up and act out their conversations. Have students in the class listen for each of the Four Cs.

Extension/Homework
Students can use the Internet to research what makes other gems valuable such as emeralds or rubies. Have students share what they learned with the class.

 Go to www.mynorthstarlab.com for *Notetaking* and *Academic Skills Practice*.

③FOCUS ON SPEAKING

A VOCABULARY

◀ SKILLS

Review vocabulary from Listenings One and Two; apply vocabulary to a new context—a conversation; expand vocabulary by understanding definitions from context; use new vocabulary in discussion.

✪ REVIEW   Suggested Time: 15 minutes

1. Look at the list of vocabulary items in the box and have students practice pronouncing each one after you. Next, go over the first item as a class. Then have students work individually to complete the activity.

2. Go over the answers as a class. Then have students practice the conversation with a partner.

Expansion/Homework
Have students cover the box of vocabulary items. Read the conversation with words filled in and have students try to complete the activity. Once you have read the conversation, let students compare answers before you read the conversation again. Then go over the answers with the class.

✪✪ EXPAND   Suggested Time: 15 minutes

 Go to www.mynorthstarlab.com for *Expand*.

1. Write *Blood Diamond* on the board. Ask if students are familiar with the movie. If so, let them summarize the story. If not, ask students what they think the title of the movie means.

2. Have students listen and read along. Encourage them to pay attention to the boldfaced words, and underline any other words they may not be familiar with.

3. Have students work in pairs to complete the matching exercise. Encourage students to use context to find the meaning. Show them an example: *They are*

heartless. They care only about themselves. Ask, *Do heartless people care about others, or only about themselves?* Explain that using context means looking at other information around the word, in the same sentence or a nearby sentence.

4. Bring the class together and ask individual students to share their answers. Then read the words and phrases aloud and have students repeat after you.

VOCABULARY EXPANSION: Vocabulary Practice

Tell students that it is important to practice vocabulary to remember it. Set aside some time each week for students to engage in short, fun practice sessions, adding vocabulary from each unit to recycle and build retention. You can use the following walk-around activity to give students an opportunity to practice vocabulary:

1. Divide the class into two groups of equal number of students. Give each student in one group an index card with a vocabulary word. Give each student in the other group an index card with the definition.

2. Begin the walk around with students exchanging cards when you call stop. On the fourth stop students should find their match, raise their cards to be checked, and put a sentence on the board if they are correct.

3. Then have students make their own flash cards with words that are still challenging.

✪ CREATE

Suggested Time: 15 minutes

1. Have students get into small groups of three or four. Have them read the questions and take turns answering. If students don't need that much structure, encourage a more open discussion. Move around the room and make sure each student speaks.

2. If time allows, ask for volunteers to share their answers with the class.

📁 Go to www.mynorthstarlab.com for additional *Vocabulary* practice.

✪✪ B GRAMMAR: The Simple Present

📁 Go to www.mynorthstarlab.com for *Grammar Chart* and *Exercise 2.*

◖ SKILLS

Learn the simple present and complete a conversation with the appropriate verb.

Suggested Time: 20 minutes

1. Have volunteers read the sentences in **Exercise 1** aloud. Then have students identify the verbs that end in *-s* by underlining them. Next, have them find the negatives and circle those verbs. Finally, have them check the *yes / no* question. Go over the answers with the class.

2. Ask individual students to read the explanations and the examples in the chart. Assist students with any pronunciation difficulties by having the whole class repeat after you. Pay special attention to final -s and the three sounds /s/, /z/, /es/.

3. Look at the photo with the class. Explain that the people are at the Tower of London where they will see the Crown Jewels. Ask students what they think Bob and Katelyn will learn.

4. Have students work individually to complete **Exercise 2** and compare their answers with a partner's. Finally, go over the answers as a class.

Expansion/Homework
(1) You can assign Exercise 2 for homework and check answers in class. (2) For further practice, offer exercises from *Focus on Grammar 1,* 2nd Edition or Azar's *Basic English Grammar,* 3rd Edition. See the Grammar Book References on page 223 of the student book for specific units and chapters.

 Go to www.mynorthstarlab.com for additional *Grammar* practice.

C SPEAKING

◖SKILLS

Practice -s endings; make suggestions; integrate the concepts, vocabulary, grammar, pronunciation, and function from the unit to complete a role play.

⊙⊙ PRONUNCIATION: -S Endings for Present Tense

Suggested Time: 25 minutes

1. Have students listen to the sentences in **Exercise 1**. Have them focus on the final -s sound. Explain the present tense -s has three sounds. Sometimes it is a final sound, and sometimes it is a new syllable. Read the explanation with the class. Then have students listen again and pay attention to each underlined verb to determine if the -s ending is a final sound or a syllable.

2. Go over the chart with the class. Read each example aloud and have students repeat. You can divide the class into smaller groups as you practice pronunciation so you can hear individual students better. Ask for more examples for each category. Write them on the board.

3. Play the conversation in **Exercise 2** and have students repeat. Then have students work with a partner and practice reading the conversation. Have them switch roles and practice again.

4. Have students complete **Exercise 3** individually. When done, have them compare their answers with a partner's. Then go over the answers as a class. Finally, have pairs take turns reading the sentences.

5. Have students work in pairs to complete **Exercise 4**. Tell them to use the example as a guide. Move around the room and offer assistance as necessary.

✪✪ FUNCTION: Making Suggestions

Suggested Time: 25 minutes

1. Explain to students that there are specific phrases they can use in a conversation to make a suggestion. Sometimes a suggestion is way to express what you want to do. For example, if you are at a party with some friends and you are tired, you might say, "Let's go home," but what you are really saying is, "I want to go home."

2. Go over the chart with the class. Read as students follow along. Then go over pronunciation of the phrases. Ask for volunteers to make some suggestions for the class. Encourage them to have fun.

3. Have students work individually to choose the correct suggestion in **Exercise 1**. Go over the answers with the class and then have students practice in pairs.

4. Working with the same partner, have students complete **Exercise 2**. Then call on pairs to read their completed conversation to the class.

5. Go over the instructions for **Exercise 3**. Have pairs think of a situation and make a short conversation using the phrases for suggestions. You can brainstorm some situations such as going out to dinner, going to the movies, etc. Give students a few minutes to prepare and practice their role plays. Then call on pairs to present their conversations for the class.

✪✪✪ PRODUCTION: Role-Play a Conversation

Suggested Time: 40–50 minutes

If you wish to assign a different speaking task than the one in this section, see page 81. The alternative topics relate to the theme of the unit but may not target the same grammar, pronunciation, or function taught in the unit.

1. Explain that the groups will act out a role play. Go over the information in the task box with the class.

2. For Steps 1 and 2, divide the class into groups of four. Have students decide which two will want to keep the bracelet and which two will not want to keep it. Take a moment to brainstorm reasons on both sides. Make a short list.

3. In Step 3, have students create a conversation and practice it for a few minutes. Encourage students to use vocabulary from the unit as well as phrases for making suggestions. Students should continue until they reach a consensus.

4. Have groups perform for the class. As other students listen, have them write down the reasons given on both sides. When done, have a discussion about which reason they think was best on both sides. (Step 4)

Link to *NorthStar: Reading and Writing 1*

Have students do the production activity again, but this time the found object is not something of obvious value, such as a diamond bracelet. One student recognizes the item as valuable (such as stamps or an antique) because he or she is a collector. Have students incorporate the vocabulary and concepts from Unit 4 as they do the role play.

○ ALTERNATIVE SPEAKING TOPICS

These topics give students an alternative opportunity to explore and discuss issues related to the unit theme.

○ RESEARCH TOPICS

Suggested Time: 20–30 minutes in class

1. Have students turn to page 217. Review the instructions for the activity with the class.

2. Have students choose an activity and conduct their research. Students can work in pairs to complete the research.

3. In class, have students form groups with other students who did the same research. Have them compare their findings. Then have groups present their most interesting information to the class.

 Go to www.mynorthstarlab.com for *Student Speaking Models, Integrated Task, Video Activity, Internet Activity,* and *Unit 4 Achievement Test.*

Together Is Better

OVERVIEW

Theme: Strength in numbers

This unit focuses on the topic of Alzheimer's disease and a support system for people with the disease. Students examine the advantages of a writers' support group that works with Alzheimer's patients to help keep memories alive.

Listening One: *I Remember* is an Alzheimer's Family Meeting, in which a psychologist explains a support group he started for people with Alzheimer's where members write and share their stories.

Listening Two: *Elsa's Story* is a narrative by an Alzheimer's patient.

Critical Thinking

Interpret the title of the unit
Describe a photograph
Recall information
Activate prior knowledge
Infer word meaning from context

Infer information not explicit in the listening
Hypothesize outcomes
Evaluate issues related to Alzheimer's disease
Rank personal preferences

Listening

Predict content
Listen for main ideas
Identify supporting details
Infer speakers' opinions
Listen to a narrative

Organize and synthesize information from the listenings
Classify sounds
Listen to and evaluate student presentations

Speaking

Express opinions
Share personal experiences
Express personal preferences

Interview a classmate
Practice interrupting politely to ask a question
Make a poster presentation

Vocabulary

Use context clues to find meaning
Define words
Use idiomatic expressions

Grammar

Like to, want to, need to

Pronunciation

/ey/ and /ɛ/

MyNorthStarLab
Readiness Check, Background and Vocabulary, Listenings One and Two, Notetaking and Academic Skills Practice, Vocabulary and Grammar, Achievement Test

NorthStar: Reading and Writing 1
Unit 5 deals with the Guardian and Urban Angels and how they help at-risk kids.

Go to www.mynorthstarlab.com for the MyNorthStarLab *Readiness Check.*

FOCUS ON THE TOPIC

❙ SKILLS

Interpret a photograph; predict content; use prior knowledge; infer the meaning of new vocabulary from context.

✷✷✷ Ⓐ PREDICT

Suggested Time: 5 minutes

1. Have students look at the title of the unit and the picture. Ask the class what the title means. Ask some follow up questions about the title such as: *Together is better than what? Why? What can the people in the picture do together that they can't do alone?*

2. Have students look at the picture and describe the people. Who are they? What are they doing? For some follow up questions, ask if any of the people remind them of people they know. If so, what does it make them think about?

✷✷ Ⓑ SHARE INFORMATION

Suggested Time: 20 minutes

1. Explain to students that they are going to test their memory. Take an informal poll of the class: Ask students to raise their hands if they think they have a good memory or a bad memory. Tell them to remember how they answered.

2. Have students study the cartoon and discuss it with a partner (**Exercise 1**). Then have students look at the cartoon for one minute then close their books and draw everything they remember (**Exercise 2**). When done, have students compare their pictures with another student's and discuss the questions in **Exercise 3**.

3. Bring the class together and ask students if they agree with their earlier response to the informal poll. Then discuss the questions in **Exercise 4** with the class. Be sure to write *Alzheimer's disease* on the board and review it for pronunciation. If students are unfamiliar with the disease, explain it is a disease that affects people's memory.

4. For follow up questions, consider: Do students notice any patterns in the kinds of things they remember or forget? Do they think there are reasons why they remember some things and not others?

Go to www.mynorthstarlab.com for *Background and Vocabulary*.

Suggested Time: 25 minutes

1. Explain that students will read and listen to an advertisement about the Alzheimer's Organization and a support group. Ask students if they know anything about the disease that wasn't mentioned in the previous activity. Ask what they think people might do in a support group.

2. Have students read while they listen to the advertisement in **Exercise 1** paying special attention to the boldfaced words and underlining any other words or phrases they don't know.

3. When done, have students answer the question in **Exercise 2**. Go over the answer with the class.

4. Have students work in pairs to complete **Exercise 3**. If students are unsure of the meanings of words, have them look back at the advertisement for help. When done, go over the answers as a class.

Go to www.mynorthstarlab.com for additional *Background and Vocabulary* practice.

② FOCUS ON LISTENING

◖ SKILLS

Predict content; identify main ideas and correct false statements; listen for details; make inferences; express opinions; listen to a narrative.

✿✿✿ **A** **LISTENING ONE: I Remember**

Go to www.mynorthstarlab.com to listen to *I Remember*.

Suggested Time: 5 minutes

Listening One is an excerpt from a meeting of families of people who suffer from Alzheimer's disease with a doctor who works with Alzheimer's patients. The doctor presents how a writers' group can help patients deal with the disease.

1. Have students look at the picture and read the information. Explain that students will hear a presentation given by a doctor to families of people who have Alzheimer's disease.

2. Have students listen to the beginning of the conversation and check what they think Dr. Alan Dienstag will and won't discuss. Ask them why they chose their answers. Encourage students to take notes as they listen.

LISTENING STRATEGY: Predicting

1. Tell students that we can improve our listening comprehension by predicting information we are going to receive as we listen, and a good way to do this is with prediction questions.

2. Have students begin by writing *Support Group for People with Alzheimer's* on the left side of a T-chart, and turning that into a question to get started. Then have students add several *wh-* questions under that they think the listening will answer.

3. Once students finish listening to the conversation, have them write the answers to the questions on the right side of the chart.

✪✪✪ LISTEN FOR MAIN IDEAS
Suggested Time: 15 minutes

1. Have students listen to the complete conversation. Then have students complete **Exercise 1**. Remind students that they have to correct the false statements. When done, have students compare their answers in a small group. Encourage disagreement and discussion.

2. Go over the answers as a class. If there is any disagreement, listen to the conversation again, stopping where appropriate to resolve it.

3. Ask students if their predictions from Section 2A were correct. If not, ask students to share what they assumed.

REACHING ALL STUDENTS: Listen for Details

- **Less Proficient:** Have students create a web as they listen. Tell them to write any words or phrases they hear during the first listening. Then have small groups discuss and combine information before listening again.

- **More Proficient:** Suggest that students make a web after they listen once. Tell them to put the title in the center and details on each branch of the web.

✪✪✪ LISTEN FOR DETAILS
Suggested Time: 15 minutes

1. Elicit the difference between main ideas and details. Explain that details support the main ideas of a listening by giving specific information such as a number or description. For example, a main idea might be that there is a support group. A detail might be the specific time it meets.

2. Play the conversation again and have students complete the exercise. Then go over the answers with the whole class. Ask individual students to read the details they completed. If there is disagreement about a detail, listen again to resolve it.

Expansion/Homework
Ask students to take notes in an outline while listening. Ask them to try and complete Listen for Details from their notes alone. Then allow students to listen again to check their answers and/or fill in any gaps in the exercise.

✪✪✪ MAKE INFERENCES

1. Explain that in the following exercise students must determine the correct answers based on information from the conversation. Explain that they will not hear specific answers, but must determine the answers by inferring the information. Encourage students to take notes on why they chose their answer. Was it the tone of the voice? Word choice? What led them to choose their answer?

2. Play each excerpt, let students individually answer, and then discuss their answers in a small group. Encourage students to explain why they chose as they did. Go over the answers after each excerpt.

✪✪✪ EXPRESS OPINIONS

1. Tell students that it is now their turn to express their own opinions about the topic of support groups and specifically a writers' group.

2. Divide the class into small groups. In each group, one student will take notes on the responses. The notes do not need to be complete sentences, just ideas. Another student will report to the class. Have groups decide who will do these roles.

3. Go over the questions with the class and help students brainstorm diseases and the problems people with those diseases face.

4. Have the groups discuss the questions. Move around the room and help students as needed. When done, ask for the group reporters to report on the group's responses.

CRITICAL THINKING

Give students the following questions for discussion in small groups before discussing as a whole class:

1. What is the purpose of this conversation?

   Answer: The purpose of the conversation is to discuss Dr. Dienstag's Alzheimer's support group.

2. Who is the audience?

   Answer: The audience is family members of patients with Alzheimer's.

3. What is one characteristic of patients with Alzheimer's?

   Answer: Patients with Alzheimer's don't remember things.

4. Give two examples of support available from the writing group.

   Answer: Members can talk about their feelings and make new friends that understand them.

✪✪✪ Ⓑ LISTENING TWO: Elsa's Story

📂 Go to www.mynorthstarlab.com to listen to *Elsa's Story*.

Suggested Time: 10 minutes

Listening Two is a narrative in which one member of the writers' group, Elsa, tells her story.

1. Have students look at the pictures and identify what they see. Ask students what they think these pictures have in common. Then explain that students will hear a member of the writers' group as she tells her story.

2. Have students listen to the narrative and complete the exercise. Then ask for individual students to read their completed sentences for the class.

✪✪✪ Ⓒ INTEGRATE LISTENINGS ONE AND TWO

◖ SKILLS

Organize information from the listenings; synthesize the information in a role play.

STEP 1: Organize   **Suggested Time: 15 minutes**

1. Tell students they will now think about people who have Alzheimer's disease and the people who are in the writers' group. People with the disease lose a lot. Have students call out some things they lose. Allow for a few examples to help students get started. Then ask students to think about people in the writers' group and call out one or two examples.

2. Go over pronunciation of the phrases in the box. Be sure students understand the meaning of the word *independence*.

3. Have students work in pairs to complete the two lists. When done, bring the class back together. Go around and have each pair give one example from one list. Write the responses on the board. Continue until all the words and phrases are on the board.

STEP 2: Synthesize   **Suggested Time: 20 minutes**

1. Explain that students are going to create a role play based on the information in the lists they completed in Step 1. Tell them that they should make the conversation as natural as possible.

2. Have students work with a partner to complete the role play. Read the introduction aloud for the class. Then give students a few minutes to prepare and practice their conversations. Move around the room and provide help where necessary with pronunciation and vocabulary.

3. If time allows, invite a few pairs to come up and act out their conversations.

Link to *NorthStar: Reading and Writing 1*

If students are also using the companion text, have them read the letter to the editor on page 119 of the *Reading and Writing* strand and write a similar letter to the editor as a family member who has a relative in the Alzheimer's writers' group. Explain why the group has been beneficial.

 Go to www.mynorthstarlab.com for *Notetaking* and *Academic Skills Practice*.

③ FOCUS ON SPEAKING

A VOCABULARY

◀ SKILLS

Review vocabulary from Listenings One and Two; apply vocabulary to a new context—an information gap activity; expand vocabulary by describing likes and dislikes; use new vocabulary creatively in a conversation.

✪ REVIEW

Suggested Time: 15 minutes

1. Have students work in pairs. Explain that each student will look at a different page. Student A will look at pages 92–93 of the student book. Student B will look at page 211. The goal is for students to listen to the statement and supply the correct responses.

2. Go over the first item as a class. Then have students work individually to complete the activity. Move around the room and offer assistance as necessary.

✪✪ EXPAND

Suggested Time: 20 minutes

 Go to www.mynorthstarlab.com for *Expand Exercise 1*.

1. Have students work alone to complete the list of activities they like and dislike in **Exercise 1**. Go over the phrases that may be unfamiliar (*hang out with, by myself*).

2. When done, review the phrases in the box for expressing likes and dislikes. Explain that students can use phrases other than "I (don't) like" such as the ones in the box. Ask for volunteers to read the phrases and complete the sentences in the box.

3. Have students work in pairs and complete **Exercise 2**. Move around the room and offer assistance. Then call on individual students to list a few activities they like and dislike.

1. Tell students that a synonym is a word that has a similar meaning to another word. For example, a synonym of *bad* would be *terrible*. Explain that synonyms add variety and make writing more interesting. We often use a thesaurus to find synonyms of words.

2. Students may be asked to listen for synonyms during the listening or locate synonyms in the text for the following list of words: *narrator, author, recollections, misplace, acquaintances, bad, illness.*

   Answers: speaker, writer, memories, lose, friends, terrible, disease

✪ CREATE   Suggested Time: 15 minutes

1. Explain to students that they will ask their partner to explain their answers from the exercise in Expand. Have students work in the same pairs. Student A can choose any three of Student B's responses and ask for an explanation by asking *why.* Student B should respond using phrases from Review and Expand.

2. Ask for a volunteer to read the example with you. Then have students work in pairs, switching after each question. When done, ask for volunteers to report one response from their partner.

   Go to www.mynorthstarlab.com for additional *Vocabulary* practice.

✪✪ B GRAMMAR: *Like to, want to, need to*

Go to www.mynorthstarlab.com for *Grammar Chart* and the *Exercise.*

◀ SKILLS

Learn *like, want, need* plus the infinitive and complete a conversation with the appropriate verb and infinitive.

Suggested Time: 20 minutes

1. Ask the class, *What do you like to do?* Get several answers from students. Correct for grammar verbally as you repeat. Write one or two examples on the board. Then do the same with *want* and *need.*

2. When you have several sample sentences on the board, ask the class to identify the verbs. Underline *like, want* and *need.* Ask students if there is a second verb in the sentence. Underline the infinitive with a double line. Ask if students know what *to* + base form of the verb is called. Label it *infinitive.* Explain that the verbs *want, like* and *need* are followed by the infinitive (*to* + base form).

3. Go over the chart with the class. Elicit additional examples from students.

4. Have students work with a partner. Student A will read a statement, Student B will ask a question about the statement by filling in the blanks. Then Student A will respond. Have students alternate A and B by item. When done, call on pairs to read individual conversations.

Expansion/Homework

(1) Have students complete the fill-in portion of the exercise for homework. **(2)** For further practice, offer exercises from *Focus on Grammar 1,* 2nd Edition or Azar's *Basic English Grammar,* 3rd Edition. See the Grammar Book References on page 223 of the student book for specific units and chapters.

 Go to www.mynorthstarlab.com for additional *Grammar* practice.

C SPEAKING

◖ SKILLS

Practice /ey/ and /ɛ/; interrupt politely to ask a question; integrate the concepts, vocabulary, grammar, pronunciation, and function from the unit to create a presentation.

✹ PRONUNCIATION: /ey/ and /ɛ/

Suggested Time: 25 minutes

1. Write *may, name, they* in a column on the board. Pronounce the words. In the next column, write *yes, forget, help.* Pronounce the words. Repeat and underline the /ey/ sounds and the /ɛ/ sounds. Then pronounce the words as contrasting pairs. Explain the two sounds are close, but produced differently. Label the first column /ey/ and the second column /ɛ/.

2. Play the audio for **Exercise 1**, have students listen, and answer the question. Then go over the chart with the class.

3. Play the audio for **Exercise 2** and have students repeat the phrases. Repeat the activity until students are comfortable with the sounds.

4. Go over the instructions for **Exercise 3**. Have students listen once. Then play the audio again and have students write the sounds they hear. Finally, have students compare answers with a partner's. Play the audio again to allow students to check their answers. Go over the answers as a class. Then play the audio once more. Pause after each statement and have students repeat. Finally, have students work with a partner and take turns reading the statements and correcting each other's errors.

5. Have students complete **Exercise 4** individually. Play the conversations and have students write the words they hear. Go over the answers with the class. Then have students practice the conversations with a partner.

Expansion/Homework

For additional recognition practice, write the sounds on the board, labeling them *1* and *2*. Say a word and have students hold up the correct number to identify the sound.

✿✿ FUNCTION: Interrupting Politely to Ask a Question

Suggested Time: 20 minutes

1. Explain to students that when you want to interrupt someone who is talking to ask a question, there are phrases to use that are polite. With books closed, ask students if they know any phrases for interrupting politely. Write them on the board. Then have students open their books. Call on three students to read the conversation aloud to the class. Then go over the phrases in the box. Read each phrase aloud and have students repeat chorally. Have students add these phrases from the board that are not listed in the box.

2. Have students work in pairs to complete the activity. Each student is looking at a different page. Students use the phrases to interrupt politely and ask a question. When complete, have the class come back together and ask for a few pairs to read their conversations for the class.

✿✿✿ PRODUCTION: Presentation

Suggested Time: 45–50 minutes

If you wish to assign a different speaking task than the one in this section, see page 100. The alternative topics relate to the theme of the unit, but may not target the same grammar, pronunciation, or function taught in the unit.

1. Students now have an opportunity to create a club for their classmates to join. Students will create posters and present them to the class. Go over the task box with the class.

2. Brainstorm ideas for different types of clubs with the class. You can start with the example of the English Conversation Club. Write it on the board then add others as students offer them. Students don't have to use one of these but can if they choose. (Other ideas might be a book club, a cooking club, a movie club, etc.)

3. For Step 1, divide the class into groups of three. Have the groups choose one of the clubs or come up with one of their own. As the groups decide which club to use, have them practice interrupting politely to ask questions.

4. For Step 2, have each group design a poster to advertise the club. You might want to do a brief brainstorm of what information to include. For example, name of the club, when and where it meets, who might be interested in joining, etc. Encourage students to think about a design that will be interesting.

5. For Step 3, have students work on their presentations. Each student in the group must speak, so groups can divide up the information Encourage

students to write brief notes to help them remember, but not to script out their presentation. They want their presentations to be as natural as possible.

6. Once all groups have planned their presentations, have groups take turns presenting. As the class listens, students should raise their hands to politely interrupt and ask questions. Explain that students will vote on the best idea at the end so students should be thinking about which presentation is best and why.

7. When all groups are done, take a class poll on which presentation was best. (Step 4) Write the names of the clubs on the board and have students vote. Call on individual students as they raise their hands to vote to explain why they think that one is best.

Expansion/Homework

Have students work on their posters outside of class to develop them with graphics and color.

 Link to *NorthStar: Reading and Writing 1*

If students are also using the companion text, have them discuss the similarities between Urban Angels and the idea of a writers' group or a support group in general. How do both kinds of groups help people?

⊙ ALTERNATIVE SPEAKING TOPICS

These topics give students an alternative opportunity to explore and discuss issues related to the unit theme.

⊙ RESEARCH TOPICS

Suggested Time: 20–30 minutes in class

1. Have students turn to page 218. Review the instructions for the activity with the class. Encourage students to come up with additional questions for the interview.

2. Have students complete their interviews and write a short summary report.

3. In class, have students work in small groups to present their reports. Have other students in the group ask questions. If you have a smaller class, have students present their reports to the whole class.

 Go to www.mynorthstarlab.com for *Student Speaking Models, Integrated Task, Video Activity, Internet Activity,* and *Unit 5 Achievement Test.*

UNIT 6 Thinking Young: Creativity in Business

OVERVIEW

Theme: Business
This unit focuses on creativity in business. Students examine and discuss the concept of being creative as a way to enhance business environments and products.

Listening One: *K-K Gregory, Young and Creative* is an excerpt from a lecture, in which a 17-year-old girl talks to a college business class about her experience being an entrepreneur.

Listening Two: *A Business Class* is an excerpt from a lecture about creativity in business and how we lose a sense of creativity as adults.

Critical Thinking

Interpret pictures
Infer word meaning from context
Infer information not explicit in the listening
Evaluate business initiatives

Hypothesize another's point of view
Reach a consensus
Support opinions with reasons

Listening

Make predictions
Listen for main ideas and correct false statements
Listen for details

Interpret people's opinions and attitudes
Listen to a lecture
Organize and synthesize information from the listenings

Speaking

Share opinions
Agree and disagree with statements
Create a conversation

Interview a classmate
React to information
Role-play a business meeting

Vocabulary

Use context clues to find meaning
Define words
Use idiomatic expressions

Grammar

There is / There are, There was / There were

Pronunciation

TH: think, this

 MyNorthStarLab
Readiness Check, Background and Vocabulary, Listenings One and Two, Notetaking and Academic Skills Practice, Vocabulary and Grammar, Achievement Test

 NorthStar: Reading and Writing 1
Unit 6 focuses on large chain stores and how they are driving small family owned businesses out of business.

56

①FOCUS ON THE TOPIC

◖SKILLS

Interpret cartoons; predict content; use prior knowledge; infer the meaning of new vocabulary from context.

✪✪✪ Ⓐ PREDICT

Suggested Time: 10 minutes

1. Look at the cartoons as a class and have students discuss what they see in each picture. Have students answer questions 1 and 2. Ask students to compare the two pictures and ask how they think each situation might make employees feel about work and why.

2. Ask students to answer question 3. Have them offer some examples of "thinking young" from experience or explain what they think it means.

3. Ask students to reflect on any work experience they may have had and how they felt at work. Have students describe the environment of their workplace and how it made them feel.

✪✪ Ⓑ SHARE INFORMATION

Suggested Time: 15 minutes

1. Write *creative* on the board and go over the explanation in the book with the class. Students may be familiar with the word *create* so begin there if they don't know *creative*. Explain it is an adjective, so it is used to describe someone. Have students raise their hands if they feel they are creative, and have them briefly describe.

2. Ask students to remember when they were children and how they were creative (make believe, dress up, painting, drawing, etc.). Then have students work alone to complete **Exercise 1**. Encourage them to add other ideas. When done, have students work in groups of four to share their ideas.

3. Have students complete **Exercise 2**. Start by going over the words for pronunciation and meaning, and allow students to use a dictionary if necessary. When students have completed the exercise, have them share their answers in their groups. Then bring the class back together and allow students to volunteer some of their answers.

Expansion/Homework

Have students bring in examples of ways they are creative now and describe them to the class.

 C BACKGROUND AND VOCABULARY

Go to www.mynorthstarlab.com for *Background and Vocabulary.*

Suggested Time: 25 minutes

1. Ask students to consider the average work environment. Brainstorm places of work (offices, schools, hospitals, etc.). Ask students how creative they think people are at work.

2. Explain that, in **Exercise 1**, students will read an article from a business magazine. Have students read the title then discuss reasons why companies might want employees to be more creative (employees will enjoy work more, will be more productive, might come up with good products, etc.). Then ask students to guess how companies might get their employees to be more creative.

3. Have students read as they listen. Encourage students to pay attention to the boldfaced words, and underline any other words or phrases they may not know.

4. When done, have students work with a partner to complete **Exercise 2**. Have students point out where they found the information. Then go over the answers. Ask students if their predictions before they read and listened were correct.

5. Have students work in pairs to complete **Exercise 3**. When done, go over the answers as a class.

Go to www.mynorthstarlab.com for additional *Background and Vocabulary* practice.

 2 FOCUS ON LISTENING

◖ SKILLS

Predict content; identify main ideas and correct false statements; listen for details; make inferences; express opinions; listen to a lecture.

LISTENING ONE: K-K Gregory, Young and Creative

📁 Go to www.mynorthstarlab.com to listen to *K-K Gregory, Young and Creative.*

Suggested Time: 5 minutes

Listening One is an excerpt from a guest speaker lecture given by a young and successful business owner. The style is somewhat informal.

1. Have students listen to the beginning of the lecture. Encourage them to take notes. Then have students answer the questions.

2. Go over the answers with the class. Ask students to say why they chose their answers.

LISTENING STRATEGY: Anticipation Guide

Create background knowledge for students by making a statement for them to consider. For example, on the topic of creativity, the statement might be, "Creative people are born. You cannot learn to be creative." Engage in a class discussion for students to express their opinions.

✪✪✪ LISTEN FOR MAIN IDEAS

Suggested Time: 10 minutes

1. Have students listen to the complete conversation and complete **Exercise 1.** Remind them to correct the false statements. Go over the answers as a class.

2. Ask students if their predictions from Section 2A were correct. If not, ask students to share what they assumed.

✪✪✪ LISTEN FOR DETAILS

Suggested Time: 15 minutes

1. Elicit the difference between main ideas and details. Explain that details support the main ideas of a listening by giving specific information such as a number or description. For example, a main idea might be that K-K made her first pair of Wristies at a young age. A detail might be her age.

2. Play the lecture again and have students complete the exercise. Then go over the answers with the whole class. Ask individual students to read the correct details. If there is disagreement about a detail, listen again to resolve it.

Expansion/Homework

Ask your students to take notes while listening and try and complete both exercises using their notes alone. Then allow them to listen again to check their answers and/or fill in any gaps in the exercises.

✪✪✪ MAKE INFERENCES

Suggested Time: 10 minutes

1. Explain that in the following exercise students must determine the correct answers based on information from the conversation. Explain that they will

not hear specific answers, but must determine the answers based on what the speakers say.

2. Have students work individually. Play the first excerpt and have students choose the answer. Then have them read the answer and explain their choice. Go over each excerpt before going on to the next, encouraging discussion.

REACHING ALL STUDENTS: Make Inferences

- **Less Proficient:** Have students work with a partner to complete the exercise.

- **More Proficient:** Challenge students to cite a specific word or words that point to the correct answers.

✪✪✪ EXPRESS OPINIONS

Suggested Time: 20 minutes

1. Tell students that it is now their turn to express their own opinions about K-K Gregory and her Wristies.

2. Divide the class into small groups. In each group, one student will take notes on the responses. Another student will report to the class. Have groups decide who will do these roles.

3. Have the groups complete the list in **Exercise 1**. When done, ask for the group reporters to report on the group's list.

4. Have the groups answer the questions in **Exercise 2**. The note taker should take notes.

5. When done, have the group reporters share their group's ideas to the class. Encourage groups to only report on ideas not reported on by the previous groups when they respond. This ensures students are listening.

CRITICAL THINKING

Give students the following questions for discussion in small groups before discussing as a whole class:

1. How many years has K-K Gregory been in business?

   Answer: She has been in business for seven years.

2. What are Wristies?

   Answer: Wristies are long gloves with no fingers.

3. How does the audience feel about K-K Gregory?

   Answer: They are impressed and admire her.

4. How do you feel about the advice given by K-K Gregory?

   Answers will vary, but students should support their opinions with information from the listening and from their own experience.

✪✪✪ B LISTENING TWO: A Business Class

📁 Go to www.mynorthstarlab.com to listen to *A Business Class*.

Suggested Time: 20 minutes

Listening Two is a business class lecture about creativity and how adults can learn from children on how to be creative. Students are encouraged to think about ways to be more creative.

1. Explain that students will hear an excerpt from a lecture. Have students listen to the discussion and complete **Exercise 1**. Go over the answers as a class.

2. Ask students what they think about professor Ray's comments about creativity in childhood and the loss of it in adulthood. Do they agree? Why?

3. Now explain that in **Exercise 2**, students will have an opportunity to try the activity for themselves. Have students listen again and follow the instructions. Then have students work in pairs to tell their story. When done, invite several students to share their stories with the class.

✪✪✪ C INTEGRATE LISTENINGS ONE AND TWO

◖ SKILLS

Organize information from the listenings in a chart; synthesize the information in a role play.

STEP 1: Organize

Suggested Time: 10 minutes

1. Point to the chart and explain that students will think about the lessons K-K had to teach. Read the lessons as listed. Then have students look at the chart and decide which part of K-K's story taught which lesson. Complete the first one with the class.

2. Have students complete the exercise. Move around the room and offer assistance. Replay relevant portions of the lectures if necessary. Then go over the answers as a class.

STEP 2: Synthesize

Suggested Time: 20 minutes

1. Read the instructions with the class. Then divide the class into pairs to complete the exercise.

2. Explain that students are going to create a role play based on the information in the chart they completed in Step 1. Tell them that they should make the conversation as natural as possible. Give students a few minutes to prepare and practice their conversations. Move around the room and provide help where necessary with pronunciation and vocabulary.

3. When all students are finished, invite a few pairs to come up and act out their conversation for the class.

Link to NorthStar: Reading and Writing 1

Students could discuss the following questions about the role of creativity in large companies: *Blockbuster is a successful business. Is it successful because it is creative? Can big companies be as creative as small companies? Why or why not?*

 Go to www.mynorthstarlab.com for *Notetaking* and *Academic Skills Practice*.

③FOCUS ON SPEAKING

Ⓐ VOCABULARY

❙ SKILLS

Review vocabulary from Listenings One and Two; apply vocabulary to a new context—a descriptive paragraph; expand vocabulary by learning and using idiomatic expressions; use new vocabulary creatively by conducting an interview.

✪ REVIEW

Suggested Time: 10 minutes

 Go to www.mynorthstarlab.com for *Review*.

1. Look at the list of vocabulary items in the box and have students practice pronouncing each one after you. Allow enough repetition for problem words.

2. Have students look at the picture while you explain that Brent Simmons is another young, creative business owner. Explain that students will read his story. Go over the first item as a class. Then have students work individually to complete the exercise.

3. Go over the answers as a class and then ask for volunteers to read the story aloud for the class.

4. Ask students what they think of Brent Simmons and his idea. Have a short discussion.

Expansion/Homework

When students are finished with this section, you may want to play a quiz game in which you ask two competing teams the definitions of words learned in the unit.

✪✪ EXPAND

Suggested Time: 20 minutes

1. Ask students what kinds of classes or opportunities they think could help employees be more creative. Some ideas they might think of are art classes, a gym at work, etc.

2. Explain that in **Exercise 1** students will read and listen to a paragraph about creativity classes. Have students listen once, then listen again paying attention to the boldfaced words. Then ask students to paraphrase what they heard.

3. Go over the boldfaced words for pronunciation and meaning. Ask questions to help students understand meaning. You can ask an example question (*Is* increase *to add to or take from? Is a* perk *something you are given or is it taken from you? How do you know?*)

4. Have students work in pairs to complete **Exercise 2**. When done, bring the class back together. Ask one of the questions and have a volunteer answer it. Then have that student ask the next question and another student respond. Continue until done.

VOCABULARY EXPANSION: Semantic Features

1. List the vocabulary words from the unit on the board. Develop a semantic features chart. Headings can include: words that are related, words with two syllables, words with a prefix, words with a suffix, words with less than six letters, words that are adjectives, etc.

2. As a group, analyze the first word on the list for each of the categories. Next, have groups form heir own semantic map and categorize the remaining words on the list.

✪ CREATE

Suggested Time: 15 minutes

Go over the instructions with the class. Then have students move around the room and interview each other. Remind students to use the vocabulary from Review and Expand. When done, ask for volunteers to report on one student.

 Go to www.mynorthstarlab.com for additional *Vocabulary* practice.

✦✦ B GRAMMAR: *There is / There are, There was / There were*

 Go to www.mynorthstarlab.com for *Grammar Chart* and *Exercise 2*.

◖ SKILLS

Learn the present and past tense of *there is / there are* and complete an interview with the appropriate tense.

Suggested Time: 20 minutes

1. Read the conversation in **Exercise 1** aloud with two other students. Then have students underline *there are, there was, there were, there weren't*. Have students identify which is past and present and which is singular. Finally, have students find and underline *are there* and *were there*. Go over the answers with the class.

2. Go over the chart with the class. Ask individual students to read the explanations and the examples. Assist students with any pronunciation difficulties by having the whole class repeat after you.

3. Have students work alone to fill in the interview in **Exercise 2**. Go over the answers as a class. Then have students work with a partner to take turns reading the interview.

Expansion/Homework

(1) You can assign Exercise 2 for homework and check answers in class. (2) For further practice, offer exercises from *Focus on Grammar 1*, 2nd Edition or Azar's *Basic English Grammar*, 3rd Edition. See the Grammar Book References on page 223 of the student book for specific units and chapters.

 Go to www.mynorthstarlab.com for additional *Grammar* practice.

C SPEAKING

◀ SKILLS

Practice pronunciation of *th*; practice phrases for reacting to new information; integrate the concepts, vocabulary, grammar, pronunciation, and function from the unit to role-play a business meeting.

∞ PRONUNCIATION OF *TH*: *think, this*

Suggested Time: 15 minutes

1. Write some sample words on the board in two columns, for example, *they, thanks, mother, anything*. Underline the *th* sound and explain that *th* has two sounds. Explain that *they* and *mother* are produced using your voice and *thanks* and *anything* are voiceless (no voice). Demonstrate the two sounds for the class.

2. Have students read the sentence and answer how many words with *th* they can identify. Call on volunteers to share their answers with the class. Then go over the information in the chart with the class. Give students ample opportunity to practice pronouncing the sounds.

3. Have students underline the words with *th* in **Exercise 1** and read the words aloud to a partner. Then play the audio and have students repeat.

4. Have students work with a partner to complete **Exercise 2**. Move around the room and help with vocabulary and pronunciation.

Expansion/Homework

Do some more recognition practice by having students hold up one finger for the voiced sound and two for the voiceless. Repeat some words and have them respond with the proper number.

✪✪ FUNCTION: Reacting to Information

Suggested Time: 15 minutes

1. Explain to students that while having a conversation, it is often expected to show interest in what the person is saying.

2. Read the explanation and the information in the chart. Read the phrases aloud, have students repeat after you, and then have volunteers read the example conversations. Help with pronunciation as necessary.

3. Look at the picture of Google's headquarters. Ask students what they know about Google (search engine, large, successful, etc.). Have students guess what kind of company Google is and why they think that. Are the employees allowed to be creative? Do students think the working conditions at Google are good? Why? Then have students describe what they see. Ask the class if it is interesting, surprising, or unusual.

4. Have students work in pairs to complete the exercise. When complete, have the class come back together. Read one statement and ask for a volunteer to respond. Repeat for all statements.

✪✪✪ PRODUCTION: Role-Play

Suggested Time: 45–50 minutes

If you wish to assign a different speaking task than the one in this section, see page 122. The alternative topics relate to the theme of the unit, but may not target the same grammar, pronunciation, or function taught in the unit.

1. Go over the information in the task box with the class. You might want to review the information about Google from the Function section.

2. For Step 1, divide the class into three equal groups. Explain each group is different and has a different task—Group 1 are Google office designers, Group 2 are employees from Google's California office, and Group 3 are employees from Google's New York office.

3. Go over the list of perks with the class. Make sure students understand the meaning of each. Then have each group complete Step 2, performing its task. Have the office designer group look at the perks at each of the Google offices. The goal is to ask employees about the perks available. Students should generate a list of questions to ask about the perks. Meanwhile, have the two groups of employees review the list of perks and think of the advantages of each perk. Students can keep notes to help them later.

4. When all the groups have completed the task, mix the groups up so each group has at least one of each role. (Step 3) Each group should assign a note taker to keep a list of perks they decide on and a reporter to speak for the group.

5. For Step 4, have the groups begin their meetings to choose the perks they want in their office. The employees can refer to their notes. The designer should start the meeting by asking the first question. For each perk, the employees should

explain why it is good. The designer can ask follow-up questions and show reactions to the information.

6. When done, have the note takers from each group write the list of perks they chose on the board. The reporter will go over the list and explain the ideas. Finally, have the whole class decide on one list for the Google office. (Step 5)

Expansion/Homework
Prior to completing this activity, have students research Google on the Internet to learn more about the company and use the information in the Production task.

 Link to *NorthStar: Reading and Writing 1*
Have students brainstorm what the work environment would be like in a small, family owned business versus a large chain store. Then have students write a short essay comparing the two workplaces.

✪ ALTERNATIVE SPEAKING TOPICS

These topics give students an alternative opportunity to explore and discuss issues related to the unit theme.

✪ RESEARCH TOPICS

Suggested Time: 20–30 minutes in class

1. Have students turn to page 219. Review the instructions for the activity with the class. Then have students choose which activity they will want to complete.

2. Have students complete the activity at home and write a short summary report.

3. In class, have students work in small groups to present their reports. Have other students in the group ask questions.

 Go to www.mynorthstarlab.com for *Student Speaking Models, Integrated Task, Video Activity, Internet Activity,* and *Unit 6 Achievement Test.*

UNIT 7
Planting Trees for Peace

67

Go to www.mynorthstarlab.com for the MyNorthStarLab *Readiness Check*.

①FOCUS ON THE TOPIC

◖ SKILLS

Label an illustration; predict content; use prior knowledge; infer the meaning of new vocabulary from context.

✪✪✪ A PREDICT

Suggested Time: 10 minutes

1. Have students look at the title of the unit and discuss the meaning. Ask students if they think planting trees can help bring peace. If so, how?

2. Have students look at the picture and describe what they see. Encourage them to use the words in the box. Then have students label the illustration. When done, go over the words, writing the answers on the board.

3. Discuss questions 2 and 3 with the class. Encourage students to give examples.

✪✪ B SHARE INFORMATION

Suggested Time: 15 minutes

1. Look at the pictures as a class. Have students describe what they see and where they think it is. Help with any vocabulary that is difficult, writing words on the board and marking for syllables and stress.

2. Have students work in small groups to complete the activity. When done, bring the class back together and go over the answers.

✪✪✪ C BACKGROUND AND VOCABULARY

📁 Go to www.mynorthstarlab.com for *Background and Vocabulary*.

Suggested Time: 25 minutes

1. Explain that students will read about a woman named Wangari Maathai. Have students look at her picture and discuss where they think she might be from. Then have students look at the picture of the book. Explain it is an autobiography. Write the word on the board. Explain it is a story about Wangari's life that she herself wrote. Ask students to guess what kinds of things she wrote about. Some ideas might be her childhood, her adult life, her work, her family, etc.

2. Have students listen to the excerpt in **Exercise 1** once, without reading along. Then, play the first part (my childhood) as students read along. Have students pay special attention to the boldfaced words and underline any other words they are not familiar with. When done, have students paraphrase what they heard and read. Continue this way for each section. If time permits, play the whole selection one more time all the way through as students read along.

3. Have students work in pairs to complete **Exercise 2**. Encourage students to look back at the selection to help them determine meanings. Have pairs switch roles after item 5. Then go over the answers as a class.

Go to www.mynorthstarlab.com for additional *Background and Vocabulary* practice.

FOCUS ON LISTENING

◀ SKILLS

Predict content; identify main ideas and arrange events in chronological order; listen for details; make inferences; express opinions; listen to a presentation and correct false statements.

✪✪✪ Ⓐ LISTENING ONE: Wangari Maathai and the Green Belt

 Go to www.mynorthstarlab.com to listen to *Wangari Maathai and the Green Belt.*

Suggested Time: 5 minutes

In Listening One, students learn about an organization called the Green Belt and the woman who started it, Wangari Maathai.

1. Have students listen to the beginning of the show. Encourage them to take notes. Then have students answer the questions.

2. Go over the answers with the class. Ask students to say why they chose their answers.

✪✪✪ LISTEN FOR MAIN IDEAS   **Suggested Time: 15 minutes**

1. Have students listen to the entire show and complete **Exercise 1**. Go over the answers with the class.

2. Ask students if their predictions from Section 2A were correct. If not, ask students to share what they assumed.

Expansion/Homework
This audio segment is long. You might want to pause after each section and have students take notes or outline the section.

LISTENING STRATEGY: Creating a Timeline

Before you assign the exercise in Listen for Main Ideas, have students create a map of their life detailing significant events. Begin by asking students to make notes in sequential order of events in their life. Students will then draw a representation of these significant events along the road map of their life. The path may have ups and downs and twists and turns as reflected by the events.

✪✪✪ LISTEN FOR DETAILS   Suggested Time: 15 minutes

Play the show again and have students complete the exercise. Then go over the answers with the whole class. Ask individual students to read the details they completed. If there is disagreement about a detail, listen again to resolve it.

REACHING ALL STUDENTS: Listen for Details

- **Less Proficient:** Have students listen to the audio and record what they heard on a timeline. After the recording, students team with a partner to discuss the information and add details to their charts.

- **More Proficient:** Have students listen to the recording and reflect on what they heard. After the recording, students team with a partner to discuss the information. Encourage them to question and make personal connections to their own lives.

✪✪✪ MAKE INFERENCES   Suggested Time: 15 minutes

1. Explain that in the following exercise students must determine the correct answers based on information from the conversation. Explain that they will not hear specific answers, but must determine the answers based on what the speaker says.

2. Have students work individually or in pairs. Play the first excerpt and have students choose an answer. Then have them read the answer and explain their choice. Go over each excerpt before going on to the next. Encourage discussion.

✪✪✪ EXPRESS OPINIONS   Suggested Time: 15 minutes

1. Tell students that it is now their turn to express their own opinions about the Green Belt organization and Wangari Maathai.

2. Divide the class into small groups. In each group, one student will take notes on the responses. The notes do not need to be complete sentences, just ideas. Another student will report to the class. Have groups decide who will do these roles.

3. Have the groups discuss the questions. When done, ask for the group reporters to share their group's responses with the class.

CRITICAL THINKING

Give students the following questions for discussion in small groups before discussing as a whole class:

1. Where is Wangari Maathai from?

   Answer: She is from Kenya, Africa.

2. What is the money raised by Green Belt for?

   Answer: Women use the money to buy food for their children.

3. What is the main idea of Part 2?

   Answer: Kenya's need for a new government

4. What is the main idea of part 3?

   Answer: Wangari was the first African woman to receive the Nobel Peace Prize.

❖❖❖ B   LISTENING TWO: Rigoberta Menchu, a Mayan Leader

📁 Go to www.mynorthstarlab.com to listen to *Rigoberta Menchu, a Mayan Leader*.

Suggested Time: 15 minutes

Listening Two is a conversation about Rigoberta Menchu, a Mayan leader for equal rights.

1. Read the introduction with the class. Then have students look at the picture and map. Have students identify what they see and where the places are located. Write the word *Mayan* on the board and ask students if they know what it refers to. Ask them to share their ideas with the class. If they don't know, explain the Mayans are indigenous people from the area of Mexico and Guatemala. They lived there long before any explorers or conquerors arrived. Ask students if there are indigenous people in their countries and if they have the same rights as others.

2. Have students listen to the presentation. Then have students complete **Exercise 1**, correcting false statements.

3. For **Exercise 2**, have students compare their answers with a partner's. Then go over the answers as a class.

❖❖❖ C   INTEGRATE LISTENINGS ONE AND TWO

◖ SKILLS

Organize information from the listenings in a chart; synthesize the information in a role play.

STEP 1: Organize
Suggested Time: 10 minutes

1. Explain that students will compare the two leaders they learned about in Listenings One and Two. They will compare where they lived, their backgrounds, their work, and what they wanted to accomplish.

2. Have students complete the exercise and compare their answers with a classmate's. Then go over the answers with the entire class.

STEP 2: Synthesize
Suggested Time: 20 minutes

1. Have students work in pairs. Explain that students are going to create a role play based on the information in the chart they completed in Step 1. Tell them that they should make the conversation as natural as possible.

2. Give students a few minutes to prepare and practice their conversation. Move around the room and provide help where necessary with pronunciation and vocabulary.

3. When all students are finished, invite a few pairs to come up and act out their conversations.

Expansion/Homework
Encourage students to bring in pictures of leaders from their countries and talk about who they are and what they did.

 Link to *NorthStar: Reading and Writing 1*
Have students recap Wangari Maathai and Rigoberta Menchu's lives using time order words from the *Reading and Writing* strand, pages 148–149.

 Go to www.mynorthstarlab.com for *Notetaking* and *Academic Skills Practice*.

③ FOCUS ON SPEAKING

A VOCABULARY

◖ SKILLS

Review vocabulary from Listenings One and Two; expand vocabulary by learning and using idiomatic expressions; use new vocabulary creatively in a conversation.

✪ REVIEW
Suggested Time: 15 minutes

1. Look at the list of vocabulary items in the box and have students practice pronouncing each one after you. Allow enough repetition for problem words.

2. Have students work in pairs. Student A will look at page 133 of the student book. Student B will look at page 213. Complete the first item with the class as an example. When done, go over the answers as a class.

EXPAND   Suggested Time: 15 minutes

Go to www.mynorthstarlab.com for *Expand.*

1. Go over the phrases in the box in **Exercise 1** for pronunciation and meaning. Students will likely know the literal meanings of the phrases. Explain these are idiomatic uses. For example, *fight for* does not mean a physical fight and *dreamed up* also does not mean dreaming while asleep.

2. Have students complete the story. Then play the story (**Exercise 2**) and have students listen and check their answers. Finally, go over the answers with the whole class.

VOCABULARY EXPANSION: Words in Context

1. After listening to the audio, have students create a road map of the details of Wangari's life. Students create a mind map representative of the content they have heard. Pictures, symbols, and colors are used to create a sequential summary of the detailed information. Vocabulary words used in context are added. Students use the map to retell the information. Allow time for students to practice with a partner before presenting to the whole group.

2. Have the rest of the class listen and evaluate the presentations using the following rubric:

Presenter: _____
Ratings: 1 – Excellent, 2 – Satisfactory, 3 – Poor
_____ Voice
_____ Posture
_____ Eye Contact
_____ Context use of target vocabulary
_____ Total Points
Comments: _____

✪ CREATE   Suggested Time: 20 minutes

1. Have students get into small groups of three or four. Have them discuss the questions. Move around the room and help with vocabulary as needed.

2. When done, have one person from each group report on the group's responses. Encourage discussion by noticing differences or similarities in responses.

Go to www.mynorthstarlab.com for additional *Vocabulary* practice.

GRAMMAR: Simple Past Tense

 Go to www.mynorthstarlab.com for *Grammar Chart* and *Exercise 2*.

◖ **SKILLS**

Learn the simple past tense and complete a conversation.

Suggested Time: 25 minutes

1. Have students read the story in **Exercise 1** individually and underline the past tense verbs. To check answers, read the story aloud. Have students raise their hands when you read a verb in the past tense.

2. Have students work in small groups to complete the tasks following the story. When done, go over the answers as a class.

3. Have individual students read the explanation and sample sentences from the chart aloud. Elicit more examples as you go over the chart. Remind students they will need to memorize irregular forms such as *feel / felt*, etc.

4. Ask students some *yes / no* and *wh-* questions and have them answer. Continue until you are sure they understand the past tense.

5. Explain that in **Exercise 2**, students will read about another leader, Eleanor Roosevelt. Ask if any students know her, or recognize her last name. If so, let them explain.

6. Have students work alone to complete the conversation, then compare answers with another student's. When done, go over the answers as a class.

7. Have students practice the conversation in pairs. Move around the room to help with pronunciation as needed.

Expansion/Homework
For further practice, offer exercises from *Focus on Grammar 1*, 2nd Edition or Azar's *Basic English Grammar*, 3rd Edition. See the Grammar Book References on page 224 of the student book for specific units and chapters.

 Go to www.mynorthstarlab.com for additional *Grammar* practice.

C **SPEAKING**

◖ **SKILLS**

Practice the pronunciation of *-ed* endings; express similarities; integrate the concepts, vocabulary, grammar, pronunciation, and function from the unit in a role play.

✪✪ PRONUNCIATION: -ed endings

Suggested Time: 25 minutes

1. Read the explanation with students and read the passage aloud for the class. Elicit responses to the questions from students.

2. Go over the rules with the class. Read each example aloud and have students repeat chorally.

3. Have students complete **Exercise 1**. Go over the answers as a class. Then play the audio again and have students repeat the words.

4. Have students complete **Exercise 2** and then compare their answers with a partner's. Go over the answers with the class. Finally, have pairs take turns telling the story to each other.

5. Go over the instructions for **Exercise 3** with the class. Then have students work in small groups and complete the exercise. Move around the room and help with vocabulary and pronunciation.

Expansion/Homework

Have students record themselves practicing the -ed endings so they can hear themselves and learn to self correct.

✪✪ FUNCTION: Expressing Similarities

Suggested Time: 20 minutes

1. Explain to students that there are specific phrases they can use in a conversation to show one person's experience is similar to or like another's. Give some examples between yourself and students, for example: *I am a woman and Keiko is, too. Kim wasn't late this morning and Antonio wasn't either.*

2. Go over the explanations in the chart and ask for volunteers to read the example sentences. Point out the use of *was / were* for the verb *be*. Explain that when using another verb, *did* needs to be used in the second phrase (Wangari fought for democracy and Rigoberta *did*, too.) Explain *did* means *fought for democracy* in this sentence. Finally, point out *too* is used to show similarities with positive statements (*Wangari is a woman and Rigoberta is, too.*) and *either* is used with negative statements (*Wangari didn't give up and Rogoberta didn't either.*).

3. Have students work in pairs to complete the exercise. Student A starts by reading a fact from the chart. Student B responds. Then students switch roles. Have students continue until all facts have been used.

4. Bring the class back together and state a few facts asking for volunteers to respond.

✪✪✪ PRODUCTION: Role-Play

Suggested Time: 40–50 minutes

If you wish to assign a different speaking task than the one in this section, see page 146. The alternative topics relate to the theme of the unit, but may not target the same grammar, pronunciation, or function taught in the unit.

1. Go over the task box with the class. Then review the instructions.

2. Start with Step 1, dividing the class into three groups, or allow students to choose which woman they want to be and form a group. Make sure the groups are balanced in the number of students.

3. Have the groups review the information they learned about the woman they will portray. Encourage students to look through the unit to find information. Encourage students to keep short notes, but not complete sentences. (Step 2)

4. In each group, have students write four or more questions to ask another woman about her life from another group.

5. For Step 3, have students form new groups, including at least one person from group A, B, and C. In the new groups, have one student begin by describing her life. Other students listen and respond if they had the same experience. The student who is speaking also answers questions from the others in the group.

6. If time permits, ask for volunteers to come to the front of the class, one as each woman, and describe her life. Let the class ask questions and respond from their own experiences.

Expansion/Homework
Prior to completing this activity, have students search the Internet to learn more about the woman they will portray and use the information in the Production task.

 Link to NorthStar: Reading and Writing 1
If students are also using the companion text, you might want to have them include Charles Lindbergh and Amelia Earhart in the role plays.

✪ ALTERNATIVE SPEAKING TOPICS

These topics give students an alternative opportunity to explore and discuss issues related to the unit theme.

✪ RESEARCH TOPICS

Suggested Time: 20–30 minutes in class

1. Have students turn to pages 219–220. Review the instructions for the activity with the class. Then have students choose a person they want to find out more about.

1. Have students complete the activity at home and write a short summary report.

2. In class, have students work in small groups to present their reports. Have other students in the group ask questions.

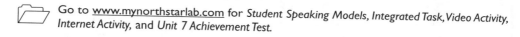 Go to www.mynorthstarlab.com for *Student Speaking Models, Integrated Task, Video Activity, Internet Activity,* and *Unit 7 Achievement Test.*

UNIT 8 Driving You Crazy

OVERVIEW

Theme: Driving problems
This unit focuses on issues related to driving. Students examine and discuss the concept of road rage and driving phobias.

Listening One: *Road Rage* is an excerpt from a traffic school lesson, in which participants discuss situations related to road rage.

Listening Two: *Driving Phobia* is a conversation between a psychologist and a person suffering from driving phobia.

Critical Thinking

Interpret a photograph
Identify common driving problems
Infer word meaning from context
Propose solutions
Support opinions with reasons
Infer information not explicit in the listening

Classify information
Hypothesize another's point of view
Analyze facts and agree on appropriate punishment
Interpret a graph

Listening

Predict feelings
Listen for main ideas
Identify supporting details
Infer speakers' attitudes, opinions, and feelings

Listen to a conversation
Organize and synthesize information from the listenings
Identify thought groups

Speaking

Share personal stories
Agree and disagree with statements
Role-play a scripted conversation
Discuss experiences

Break sentences into thought groups
Express different points of view
Discuss a case study and present a decision

Vocabulary

Use context clues to find meaning
Identify synonyms
Use idiomatic expressions

Grammar

Simple past and past progressive

Pronunciation

Thought groups

 MyNorthStarLab
Readiness Check, Background and Vocabulary, Listenings One and Two, Notetaking and Academic Skills Practice, Vocabulary and Grammar, Achievement Test

 NorthStar: Reading and Writing 1
Unit 8 focuses on the problem of traffic congestion and possible solutions.

1 FOCUS ON THE TOPIC

◖ SKILLS

Interpret a photograph; predict content; use prior knowledge; infer the meaning of new vocabulary from context.

✪✪✪ A PREDICT

Suggested Time: 5 minutes

1. Have students look at the title of the unit. Elicit meanings from students. Point out that it is an idiom (a phrase that can't be understood by understanding its parts) that means *to make or cause someone to feel frustrated;* it does not literally mean to drive or to go crazy.

2. Have the class look at the picture and discuss the questions. You might want to ask additional questions, such as: *What do you think happened right before this scene? What might happen next?*

✪✪ B SHARE INFORMATION

Suggested Time: 20 minutes

1. Read the words in the box aloud and have students repeat after you. Then have students work in pairs to complete **Exercise 1**. When done, go over the answers as a class.

2. Have students work on **Exercise 2** individually and label the illustrations. Then go over the answers with the class.

3. Have students work with a partner to discuss the questions in **Exercise 3**. Have students take notes. When done, have students share their answers with the class.

Expansion/Homework
(1) You could encourage students to enact driving problems by moving about the classroom. This can clarify driving concepts and help illustrate new vocabulary.
(2) For a written assignment, students can answer question 1 in Exercise 3 in a paragraph.

✿✿✿ C   BACKGROUND AND VOCABULARY

📁   Go to www.mynorthstarlab.com for *Background and Vocabulary.*

Suggested Time: 20 minutes

1. Write *blog* on the board and elicit the meaning from the class. Explain that a blog is a website that is like a diary. People can write about events, news, or any subject they like.

2. Have students read the blog in **Exercise 1** individually, paying special attention to the boldfaced words. Have students underline any other words or phrases they may not know.

3. Have students complete **Exercise 2** individually and then compare answers with another student's. Encourage students to point to places in the blogs that helped them understand the meaning of the words. Finally, go over the answers as a class.

📁   Go to www.mynorthstarlab.com for additional *Background and Vocabulary* practice.

②FOCUS ON LISTENING

◖ SKILLS

Predict content; identify main ideas; listen for details; make inferences; express opinions about driving problems.

✿✿✿ A   LISTENING ONE: Road Rage

📁   Go to www.mynorthstarlab.com to listen to *Road Rage.*

Suggested Time: 10 minutes

Listening One is an excerpt from a traffic school lesson. Students learn about driving problems, specifically road rage.

1. Explain that students will be listening to a traffic school class. Explain that in the United States, when people get a driving ticket, they can go to traffic school to reduce or waive the fine. In traffic school, they discuss issues related to driving.

2. Have students listen to the beginning of the lesson. Encourage them to take notes. Then have students answer the questions. Go over the answers with the class. Ask students to say why they chose their answers.

Have student groups form a panel to discuss the topic on the response card. Topics may be generic for use with any selection or specific to the text in the lesson. Panel members do not have to agree on a group response. Students may respond to a statement made by another panel member. Students may be given a token to place on their desk when they want the opportunity to speak. Limit tokens to two per person to insure all group members have the opportunity to participate.

✪✪✪ LISTEN FOR MAIN IDEAS

Suggested Time: 10 minutes

Have students listen to the complete lesson and check what each person did. Go over the answers as a class. If there is any disagreement, listen to the lesson again to resolve it.

Expansion/Homework
You could have the class discuss the following questions: *Do you ever get angry when you drive? What do you do when you get angry? Are you a safe driver when you are angry? Why or why not?*

✪✪✪ LISTEN FOR DETAILS

Suggested Time: 10 minutes

Play the lesson again and have students complete the exercise. Go over the answers with the whole class. Ask individual students to read the answers.

REACHING ALL STUDENTS: Listen for Details

• **Less Proficient:** Have students complete the exercise with a partner. Allow students to use the audioscript to complete the exercise.	• **More Proficient:** Have students correct the false statements.

✪✪✪ MAKE INFERENCES

Suggested Time: 15 minutes

1. Explain that in the following exercise students must determine the correct answers based on information from the conversation. Explain that they will not hear specific answers, but must determine the answers based on what the speakers say.

2. Have students work in small groups. Play each excerpt and let students discuss and choose the answer before going on to the next one. Encourage discussion. When done, go over the answers as a class.

✪✪✪ EXPRESS OPINIONS

Suggested Time: 15 minutes

1. Tell students that it is now their turn to express their own opinions about the topic of road rage.

2. Have students work in pairs. Have students first answer the questions individually by agreeing or disagreeing with each statement. When done, have students compare answers and explain their responses.

3. Go over the responses as a class. Emphasize that each student might have a different opinion and that there is no right or wrong answer.

CRITICAL THINKING

Give students the following questions for discussion in small groups before discussing as a whole class:

1. Explain the term *road rage*.

   Answer: Road rage means getting angry at other drivers.

2. According to the text, what are some causes of road rage?

   Answer: crowded roads, more traffic, more stress

3. What is the instructor's purpose for bringing in guest speakers?

   Answer: He wanted the class to hear true stories from real people.

4. What would you do if you were Marie's friend?

   Answers will vary, but they should reflect helping Marie control her road rage.

✪✪✪ B LISTENING TWO: Driving Phobia

Go to www.mynorthstarlab.com to listen to *Driving Phobia*.

Suggested Time: 15 minutes

Listening Two is a conversation between a psychologist and a driver suffering from a driving phobia. In the conversation, the psychologist is trying to help the driver overcome his fear.

1. Read the introduction aloud with the class. Explain that a psychologist is specially trained to help people with their problems, such as phobias (fears).

2. Have students look at the picture and explain that the man, Allen, is afraid to drive across the bridge. The other man is a psychologist, someone who is trained to help people. Ask students to describe how Allen must be feeling and what he is afraid of.

3. Have students listen to the conversation and complete the activity individually. Then go over the answers as a class. If there is disagreement, play the conversation again.

C INTEGRATE LISTENINGS ONE AND TWO

◀ SKILLS

Organize information from the listenings in a chart; synthesize the information in a role play.

STEP 1: Organize   Suggested Time: 15 minutes

1. Point to the chart and explain that students will complete the chart by writing each person's problem, where they got help, and what they learned.

2. Divide the class into pairs and have students complete the exercise. Then go over the answers with the class.

STEP 2: Synthesize   Suggested Time: 20 minutes

1. Divide the class into groups of three. Explain that students are going to create a role play based on the information in the chart they completed in Step 1. Each student will take the role of one of the drivers (John, Marie, and Allen). Tell students that they should make the role play as natural as possible.

2. Give students a few minutes to prepare and practice their role plays. Move around the room and provide help where necessary with pronunciation and vocabulary.

3. When students are finished, invite a few groups to come up and act out their role plays.

Link to *NorthStar: Reading and Writing 1*

If students are also using the companion text, have them make a list of alternate forms of transportation and then have a discussion how these alternate ways of transportation could reduce road rage and/or be helpful to people with driving phobias.

Go to www.mynorthstarlab.com for *Notetaking* and *Academic Skills Practice*.

③ FOCUS ON SPEAKING

A VOCABULARY

◀ SKILLS

Review vocabulary from Listenings One and Two; apply vocabulary to a new context—a conversation; expand vocabulary by defining new words; use new vocabulary creatively in a conversation.

✪ REVIEW
Suggested Time: 20 minutes

 Go to www.mynorthstarlab.com for *Review.*

1. Read the list of vocabulary items in the box aloud and have students repeat chorally. Divide the class into smaller groups for repetition so you can hear all students.

2. Have students work individually to complete **Exercise 1**. When done, play the conversation (**Exercise 2**) and have students self-correct. Bring the class back together and ask individual students to provide answers.

3. For **Exercise 3**, have students role-play the conversation with a partner.

✪✪ EXPAND
Suggested Time: 10 minutes

1. Explain that students will read about one student's experience in traffic school. Have students read the passage in **Exercise 1** individually. Then read the passage aloud as students read along.

2. Go over the pronunciation of the boldfaced words. Then have students complete **Exercise 2** individually. Encourage students to underline words that helped them understand the definitions. Go over the answers as a class.

VOCABULARY EXPANSION: Idioms

1. Explain that idioms are word combinations that have different meaning than the individual words. Explain that idioms are expressions with figurative meaning.

2. Provide the following examples of idioms and ask students to guess the meaning: *killing time, play with fire, cloud nine, going bananas, let the cat out of the bag, eye to eye, head above water, piece of cake, green thumb, early bird catches the worm.* Ask students to provide other examples and add them to the list.

3. Have student pairs select an idiom to investigate. Each team will illustrate, provide figurative and literal translations, and use the expression in a sentence. After terms are presented to the whole class, display students' work.

✪ CREATE
Suggested Time: 15 minutes

1. Have students work in pairs to discuss the questions. Move around the room to help with vocabulary and pronunciation.

2. If time allows, bring the class together and have students share responses. As responses are shared, ask if others have a similar experience. Allow students to add on.

 Go to www.mynorthstarlab.com for additional *Vocabulary* practice.

📁 Go to www.mynorthstarlab.com for *Grammar Chart* and *Exercise 2*.

◀ **SKILLS**

Learn simple past and past progressive; complete a story with the appropriate tense.

Suggested Time: 30 minutes

1. Read the sentences in **Exercise 1** with students. Then have students answer the questions. Discuss the answers with the class.

2. Ask for volunteers to read the information and the examples in the charts. Try to include as many students in the task as possible. Elicit additional examples from students, correcting for grammar as necessary by repeating the student's response using correct grammar.

3. To provide a visual comparison, draw a horizontal line on the board. Make a short line crossing it and label in *now.* Then make a single *x* on the line to the left of *now.* Label that *simple past.* Write a few examples *(forgot, honked, turned).* Then under the *x*, make a squiggly line that starts before the *x* and continues past it. Under that line, write *was driving, was following.* Write a sample sentence: *John was driving when he forgot to signal.* Show how *forgot* happened at one point in time (point to the *x*) so students use *when* but the driving continued over a longer time (point to the squiggly line). Write another example: *John was driving a truck while he was honking.* Show how both events are continuing at the same time in the past. In this example, students use *while.*

4. Ask for a few volunteers to provide sentences. Point to the timeline as they speak. Correct for grammar as necessary.

5. Have students work in small groups to complete **Exercise 2**. Encourage students to use a timeline if helpful. When done, go over the answers as a class.

6. Have students work in pairs to complete **Exercise 3**. Remind students they will present their partner's story to the class. They can take notes, but discourage writing out the full story. If students can't think of a true story, let them describe a picture in the unit or make up a story. Move around the room and offer assistance.

7. Go over the instructions and example in **Exercise 4**. Give students a few minutes to collect their notes and prepare the speech. Then call on students to present to the class. As a listening activity, have students in the class keep a list of the driving problems and students' names. When done, randomly ask students to report on a name and problem they heard about.

Expansion/Homework
(1) You might want to have students prepare their speech at home and present it the next day. (2) For further practice, offer exercises from *Focus on Grammar 1,* 2nd

Edition or Azar's *Basic English Grammar,* 3rd Edition. See the Grammar Book References on page 224 of the student book for specific units and chapters.

 Go to www.mynorthstarlab.com for additional *Grammar* practice.

Ⓒ SPEAKING

◖ SKILLS

Practice thought groups; express different points of view; integrate the concepts, vocabulary, grammar, pronunciation, and function from the unit in a case study.

✪ PRONUNCIATION: Thought Groups

Suggested Time: 20 minutes

1. Explain that with very long sentences, it can be difficult for listeners to follow. Typically speakers break the sentences up into thought groups; shorter groups of words. As speakers, students also want to be aware of thought groups so the listener can understand them better. Go over the explanation with the class.

2. Have students listen to the example sentences, making a note of the thought groups. Play the sentences a few times and then discuss with the class what the thought groups are.

3. Go over the information and examples in the chart. Read the examples aloud, dividing the sentences into thought groups as indicated. Have students repeat chorally.

4. Have students listen to the conversation in **Exercise 1**. Play the conversation a few times as students listen and repeat. Then have students practice the conversation with a partner.

5. Have students complete **Exercise 2** individually and then compare answers with a partner's. Emphasize that their thought groups may be different. If they are different, have students discuss if there is a difference in meaning. Then have students practice the sentences with their partner.

6. In **Exercise 3**, students will group more sentences together, which will allow for more natural speaking. Encourage students to draw diagrams to help them explain. Have students work in pairs to practice the sentences. When done, ask for volunteers to say a few groupings of sentences. Have the class listen for thought groups.

✺✺ FUNCTION: Expressing Different Points of View

Suggested Time: 20 minutes

1. Make a statement that will generate disagreement (for example, *Women are worse drivers than men.* Or, *It's OK to get angry when you drive.*). Use the examples to show students that there are always different ways to think about a situation, or different points of view. Explain to students that there are specific phrases they can use in a conversation to express different points of view.

2. Read the conversation in **Exercise 1** with a student. Then go over the phrases in the chart. Read each phrase aloud and have students repeat chorally.

3. Have students work in groups of four to complete **Exercise 2**. Students take turns reading the statements aloud, then each take turns offering a different point of view. Remind students there is no one right answer. Move around the room and help with pronunciation and vocabulary.

✺✺✺ PRODUCTION: Case Study

Suggested Time: 45–50 minutes

If you wish to assign a different speaking task than the one in this section, see page 167. The alternative topics relate to the theme of the unit but may not target the same grammar, pronunciation, or function taught in the unit.

1. Explain to students that they will now discuss a case study. Write *case study* on the board and ask if anyone knows the definition. Write any ideas students have. Then explain that a case study is a way to do research on a social problem. It is a way to look at one event, to try to understand why it happened, and to understand why it might be important. In this case study, students will examine parking rage. Go over the information in the task box with the class.

2. Have students look at the picture and describe what happened and how the driver feels. Then read the case facts in Step 1 aloud as students read along.

3. In Step 2, divide the class into groups of three or four. Explain that each group will decide on the punishment and then share it with the class. Each student will have to talk during the presentation, so in the groups, students must divide up the speaking tasks. Offer ways to divide the task such as: one student presents the situation, one presents the proposed punishment, one explains the reasoning for it, and one answers questions.

4. For Steps 3–4, have the groups discuss the case and reach a decision about the punishment. Then call on each group to present their decision to the class. As groups present, encourage students from other groups to ask questions. (Step 5)

⬭⬭ Link to *NorthStar: Reading and Writing 1*
You could have students write a class blog on driving problems they have seen. Have students write their entries on paper that can be posted around the class or online if you can quickly create a blog website.

⚙ ALTERNATIVE SPEAKING TOPICS

These topics give students an alternative opportunity to explore and discuss issues related to the unit theme.

⚙ RESEARCH TOPICS

Suggested Time: 20–30 minutes in class

1. Have students turn to page 220. Review the instructions for the activity with the class. Go over the questions. Encourage students to ask additional questions as well.

2. Have students conduct the interviews and write a short summary report.

3. In class, have students work in groups to present their reports. Have other students in the group ask additional questions.

 Go to www.mynorthstarlab.com for *Student Speaking Models, Integrated Task, Video Activity, Internet Activity,* and *Unit 8 Achievement Test.*

UNIT 9

Only Child— Lonely Child?

OVERVIEW

Theme: Family
This unit focuses on the topic of families and family size. Students examine and discuss the advantages and disadvantages of being an only child.

Listening One: *Changing Families* is a talk show, in which guests speak about their decision to have only one child.

Listening Two: *How Do Only Kids Feel?* is a continuation of the talk show, in which the host interviews the children about their feelings about not having a sibling.

Critical Thinking

Interpret illustrations
Conduct a survey
Infer word meaning from context
Compare families
Identify advantages and disadvantages

Infer information not explicit in the listening
Hypothesize another's point of view
Propose solutions
Interpret a graph

Listening

Predict content
Listen for main ideas
Listen for details
Correct false statements

Infer speakers' opinions and attitudes
Organize and synthesize information from the listenings
Listen to student presentations

Speaking

Ask and answer questions
Share experiences
Express opinions
Agree and disagree with statements

Act out a scripted conversation
Discuss ideas
Create a role play

Vocabulary

Use context clues to find meaning
Define words
Use idiomatic expressions

Grammar

The future with *be going to*

Pronunciation

"Going to" vs. "Gonna"

 MyNorthStarLab
Readiness Check, Background and Vocabulary, Listenings One and Two, Notetaking and Academic Skills Practice, Vocabulary and Grammar, Achievement Test

 NorthStar: Reading and Writing 1
Unit 9 focuses on the topic of large families, the rise of multiple births, and the impact a multiple birth has on a family.

Go to www.mynorthstarlab.com for the MyNorthStarLab *Readiness Check*.

FOCUS ON THE TOPIC

◀ SKILLS

Interpret illustrations; predict content; use prior knowledge; infer the meaning of new vocabulary from context.

✱✱✱ A PREDICT

Suggested Time: 5 minutes

Have students look at the pictures and describe what they see. Then discuss the questions as a class. You can ask a follow-up question such as: *Why do you think the child feels that way?*

✱✱ B SHARE INFORMATION

Suggested Time: 20 minutes

1. Ask students how many of them have one sibling. Write *siblings* on the board. Practice pronunciation and explain it means brothers and sisters. Then explain that students will now have a chance to learn about their classmates' families. Have students look at the chart in **Exercise 1** as you read the questions and explain the marking system. Explain that if the answer to number 1 is *no,* students go to question 2. Have students walk around to complete the activity.

2. When done, bring the class back together. Write the information from **Exercise 2** on the board. Ask students to raise their hands as you fill in the information.

Expansion/Homework
Have students bring in family pictures and share the names and basic information about their families (ages, where they live, what they do). This can be a small group activity or a writing activity.

✱✱✱ C BACKGROUND AND VOCABULARY

Go to www.mynorthstarlab.com for *Background and Vocabulary*.

Suggested Time: 15 minutes

1. Explain that students will read and listen to an article from a magazine *Only Child* for families with one child. Have students work individually to fill in the vocabulary in **Exercise 1**.

2. For **Exercise 2**, play the audio and have students self-correct their answers. Then call on individual students to read the answers. Write the words on the board.

📁 Go to www.mynorthstarlab.com for additional *Background and Vocabulary* practice.

FOCUS ON LISTENING

◖ SKILLS

Predict content; identify main ideas; identify details and correct false statements; make inferences; express opinions.

✪✪✪ Ⓐ LISTENING ONE: Changing Families

📁 Go to www.mynorthstarlab.com to listen to *Changing Families*.

Suggested Time: 5 minutes

Listening One is an excerpt from a TV talk show about families. Students listen to an interview with couples who choose to have only one child.

Have students listen to the beginning of the TV talk show and answer the questions. Ask them why they chose their answers. Explain to students that their answers are just predictions. Affirm each prediction as a possibility.

LISTENING STRATEGY: Skeleton Outline

1. A skeleton outline is used to introduce notetaking and text structure. Practice the strategy with a small amount of familiar material for the first experience.

2. Play the beginning of the interview, stopping at this line:
   MARK: Yeah. We decided that we were happy with our little family, and that one child was enough for us.

   Provide the following outline and ask students to complete the information as they listen:

   I. Changing _____
     A. People
       I. Maria _____
       2. _____
       3. _____
     B. Reasons for only one child
       I. married at age _____
       2. not easy raising a _____ child
       3. _____ with their little family

✪✪✪ LISTEN FOR MAIN IDEAS   Suggested Time: 10 minutes

1. Have students listen to the complete interview and complete **Exercise 1**. If necessary, play the interview again to allow students to finish.

2. Go over the answers as a class. If there is any disagreement, listen to the conversation again to resolve it.

3. When done, ask students if their predictions from Section 2A were correct. If not, ask students to share what they assumed.

✪✪✪ LISTEN FOR DETAILS   Suggested Time: 15 minutes

1. Have students listen to the interview again. Then have them complete the exercise.

2. Go over the answers with the whole class. Ask individual students to read the statements and correct the false statements. If there is disagreement about a detail, listen again to resolve it.

REACHING ALL STUDENTS: Listen for Details	
• **Less Proficient:** Have students work in pairs to complete the exercise. Allow them to use the audioscript to correct the false statements.	• **More Proficient:** Have students keep their books closed as they listen.

✪✪✪ MAKE INFERENCES   Suggested Time: 10 minutes

1. Explain that in the following exercise students must determine the correct answers based on information from the conversation. Explain that they will not hear specific answers, but must determine the answers based on what the speakers say.

2. Have students listen to each excerpt and choose the correct answer. Then have students compare answers with a classmate's before going over the answer with the class. Encourage discussion.

✪✪✪ EXPRESS OPINIONS   Suggested Time: 15 minutes

1. Tell students that it is now their turn to express their own opinions about the topic of families with only one child.

2. Have students look at the statements as you read them aloud. Elaborate on the statements. For example, in question 1, ask what age people typically become parents in their countries.

3. Have students complete the statements individually and then discuss the responses as a class. Read the statement and have students raise their hands to show agreement or disagreement. Ask for volunteers to explain their responses.

Expansion/Homework

For homework, have students choose one statement and write a pargraph explaining their position.

CRITICAL THINKING

Give students the following questions for discussion in small groups before discussing as a whole class:

1. What reason did the Carters give for only having one child?

   Answer: Their age

2. Do you agree or disagree that only children are often lonely?

   Answers will vary. Accept answers students can support.

3. Why was it a hard decision for Tom and Jenna to decide to have only one child?

   Answer: It was a hard decision because they both love kids.

4. What is your opinion of having only one child?

   Answers will vary, but students should support their opinions with information from the text and their own experience and knowledge.

✪✪✪ B LISTENING TWO: How Do Only Kids Feel?

📁 Go to www.mynorthstarlab.com to listen to *How Do Only Kids Feel?*

Suggested Time: 10 minutes

Listening Two is the continuation of the talk show about families. The host is interviewing children about their feelings about being the only child.

1. Ask students if they think the only children of the talk show guests in Listening One agree or disagree with their parents and why.

2. Explain that students will hear more of the talk show with the children of the parents who spoke in Listening One.

3. Have students listen to the show and complete the exercise as they listen. If necessary, play the interview again to allow students to finish. Then go over the answers as a class.

✪✪✪ C INTEGRATE LISTENINGS ONE AND TWO

◗ SKILLS

Organize information from the listenings in a chart; synthesize the information in a role play.

STEP 1: Organize

1. Explain that students have heard from the parents and children of families with only one child. Have a brief discussion about the advantages and disadvantages of being or having an only child.

2. Have students complete the chart and compare answers with a partner's. Then go over the answers with the entire class.

STEP 2: Synthesize

1. Have students work in pairs to complete the activity. Explain that students are going to create a role play based on the information in the chart they completed in Step 1. Tell them that they should make the conversation as natural as possible.

2. Give students a few minutes to prepare and practice their role plays. Move around the room and provide help where necessary with pronunciation and vocabulary.

3. When all students are finished, invite a few pairs to come up and act out their conversation.

 Link to *NorthStar: Reading and Writing 1*

Have students discuss the McCaughey family. Ask them what they think the McCaugheys would say about having a single-child family and what advice they would have for families who want to have more than one child.

 Go to www.mynorthstarlab.com for *Notetaking* and *Academic Skills Practice*.

③FOCUS ON SPEAKING

Ⓐ VOCABULARY

◀ SKILLS

Review vocabulary from Listenings One and Two; apply vocabulary to a new context—a conversation; learn and practice new vocabulary; use new vocabulary creatively in a conversation.

✪ REVIEW

 Go to www.mynorthstarlab.com for *Review*.

1. Read the list of vocabulary items in the box aloud and have students repeat chorally. Allow enough repetition for problem words.

2. Have students work in pairs to complete the activity, switching roles when they get to the second conversation.

3. When done, have different pairs read one set of sentences. Correct as necessary for pronunciation by repeating the correct pronunciation and having students repeat after you.

✪✪ EXPAND

Suggested Time: 15 minutes

1. Ask students if they have ever read in a magazine where readers send in letters or comments and the magazine editor responds. Explain that they will read readers' comments and responses from the editor of the *Only Child* magazine.

2. Go over pronunciation of the boldfaced words in **Exercise 1** by having students repeat after you. Then explain that Student A will read from "This is what THEY say" aloud and Student B will read from "our responses." Have students work in pairs to complete the exercise.

3. When done, have the pairs continue to work together to complete **Exercise 2**. Go over the answers as a class. Then have pairs complete **Exercise 3**. Finally, have student A read from "This is what they say" as Student B reads the appropriate response (**Exercise 4**).

VOCABULARY EXPANSION: Word Sort

Word sorting is another way to review and retain vocabulary. Engage students in manipulating the target vocabulary by asking them to sort the words into given categories:

Verbs—Action Word   Nouns—Names of Things   Adjectives—Descriptive Words

✪ CREATE

Suggested Time: 15 minutes

1. Have students work in a small group of three or four. Explain that students will discuss the ideas in the article.

2. Go over the example with the class. Explain that each student in the group should take a turn answering. Move around the room as students work, helping with vocabulary and pronunciation.

3. If time permits, bring the class together and have an open discussion of the ideas from the article.

Expansion/Homework
Have students do an Internet search for other single-child organizations or magazines and find if there are other common problems people discuss. Have students share their findings with the class.

Go to www.mynorthstarlab.com for additional *Vocabulary* practice.

✪✪ B GRAMMAR: The Future with *Be Going To*

Go to www.mynorthstarlab.com for *Grammar Chart* and *Exercise 2*.

◖ SKILLS

Learn about *be going to* to describe future events; complete a conversation with *be going to*; practice writing and answering questions with *be going to*.

Suggested Time: 25 minutes

1. Read the conversation in **Exercise 1**. Then have students answer the questions. Go over the answers as a class.

2. Go over the chart with the class. Ask individual students to read the explanations and the examples. Students may ask how *be going to* differs from *will*. Explain that *will* is used for future plans.

3. Have students complete **Exercise 2**. Go over the answers as a class. Then have students practice the conversation in pairs.

4. For **Exercise 3**, have students work in small groups of four or five. Encourage students who complete the first part quickly to write more questions. Have students place the questions in a bag and exchange it with another group. Then have students complete the activity. Walk around the room assisting with pronunciation and grammar.

Expansion/Homework

For further practice, offer exercises from *Focus on Grammar 1*, 2nd Edition or Azar's *Basic English Grammar*, 3rd Edition. See the Grammar Book References on page 224 of the student book for specific units and chapters.

Go to www.mynorthstarlab.com for additional *Grammar* practice.

C SPEAKING

◖ SKILLS

Practice pronunciation of *going to* versus *gonna*; practice phrases for agreeing and disagreeing; integrate the concepts, vocabulary, grammar, pronunciation, and function from the unit to role-play a conversation.

○○ PRONUNCIATION: "Going to" vs. "Gonna"

Suggested Time: 20 minutes

1. Read the explanation with the class and then play the audio. Have students identify how *going to* is pronounced.

2. Go over the information in the chart with students. Read the examples aloud and have students repeat chorally.

3. Go over the instructions and the example in **Exercise 1**. Then play the audio and have students complete the exercise. Go over the answers as a class. Then play the audio again, pausing after each item, and have students repeat chorally.

4. Go over the instructions for **Exercise 2**. First, have students match the phrases in column A and column B. Then divide the class into pairs and have students say their sentences to their partner. Finally, call on individual students to say some of their sentences to the class.

✪✪ FUNCTION: Agreeing and Disagreeing

Suggested Time: 20 minutes

1. Ask for volunteers to read the examples in the box for the class. Have two students read the example conversation aloud. Go over pronunciation of the phrases with the class having them repeat the phrases after you. Encourage the use of intonation to show how strong they feel.

2. Have students work in pairs to complete the exercise. Move around the room and provide assistance where necessary. When complete, have the class come back together then go around the room and have pairs read one statement and ask for the next student to agree or disagree.

✪✪✪ PRODUCTION: Role-Play

Suggested Time: 40–45 minutes

If you wish to assign a different speaking task than the one in this section, see page 189. The alternative topics relate to the theme of the unit, but may not target the same grammar, pronunciation, or function taught in the unit.

1. Explain to students that they will now conduct a role play on the topic of families. Read the description in the task box with the class then have students read about Ken, Betsy, and Katie. Discuss any vocabulary questions.

2. Divide the class into two groups. Have the groups complete the task (Group A is Ken, Group B is Betsy). Then have each student from Group A find a partner from Group B to complete the role play.

3. Bring the class back together and take a poll of the pairs' decisions. Allow for a class discussion of reasons. As each student gives a reason, other students should ask questions and agree or disagree with the reasons.

Link to *NorthStar: Reading and Writing 1*
Have students do a similar role play using the prompt from the writing activity. Divide the class into two groups—those who think there should be single-child families and those who support families with multiple children.

◐ ALTERNATIVE SPEAKING TOPICS

These topics give students an alternative opportunity to explore and discuss issues related to the unit theme.

◐ RESEARCH TOPICS

Suggested Time: 20–30 minutes in class

1. Have students turn to page 221. Review the instructions for the activity with the class.

2. Have students complete their interviews and write a short summary report.

3. In class, have students share their reports in small groups. Encourage other students in the group to ask questions.

 Go to www.mynorthstarlab.com for *Student Speaking Models, Integrated Task, Video Activity, Internet Activity,* and *Unit 9 Achievement Test.*

UNIT 10 The Beautiful Game

Theme: Sports

This unit focuses on the topic of sports and the popularity of soccer worldwide. Students examine and discuss why soccer is popular in the world, but not in the United States.

Listening One: *The Sports File* is a radio show, in which a reporter interviews people from all over the world about why they are soccer fans.

Listening Two: *America Talks* is a radio call-in show, in which callers discuss why soccer is not popular in the United States.

Critical Thinking

Interpret photographs	Infer information not explicit in the listening
Conduct a survey	Rate preferences
Activate prior knowledge	Support opinions with reasons
Infer word meaning from context	Determine the meaning of a message

Listening

Predict content	Organize and synthesize information from the
Identify main ideas	listenings
Identify details	Listen for important words
Infer speakers' intentions and attitudes	Listen to and rate student presentations
Correct false statements	

Speaking

Share experiences	Talk about sports
Express opinions about sports	Practice stressing important words
Ask and answer questions	Introduce reasons
Agree and disagree with statements	Create and present a TV ad

Vocabulary

Use context clues to find meaning
Define words
Categorize vocabulary
Use idiomatic expressions

Grammar

Should for ideas and opinions

Pronunciation

Stress on important words

 MyNorthStarLab
Readiness Check, Background and Vocabulary, Listenings One and Two, Notetaking and Academic Skills Practice, Vocabulary and Grammar, Achievement Test

 NorthStar: Reading and Writing 1
Unit 10 focuses on the topic of young people joining the world of professional sports.

Go to www.mynorthstarlab.com for the MyNorthStarLab *Readiness Check*.

①FOCUS ON THE TOPIC

◖ SKILLS

Interpret pictures; predict content; use prior knowledge; infer the meaning of new vocabulary from context.

✺✺✺ Ⓐ PREDICT

Suggested Time: 5 minutes

1. Have students look at the picture and identify the sport it depicts. Ask students if they are familiar with the sport and if they watch it and why.

2. Discuss the questions as a class. Then have students read the title of the unit and speculate what it means. Discuss with students what the unit will be about.

✺✺ Ⓑ SHARE INFORMATION

Suggested Time: 20 minutes

1. Ask students to name various sports that are popular in their countries. Write them on the board and go over pronunciation.

2. Have students mingle and survey three classmates about their favorite sport. When done, call on individual students to report on their findings to the class.

Expansion/Homework
Have students bring in pictures of famous sports figures from their countries and describe them to the class.

✺✺✺ Ⓒ BACKGROUND AND VOCABULARY

 Go to www.mynorthstarlab.com for *Background and Vocabulary*.

Suggested Time: 20 minutes

1. Ask students to raise their hands if they play or watch soccer. Ask students questions such as where they play, how many people are on one team, if people wear special uniforms, and how points are scored.

2. Have students read and listen to the presentation in **Exercise 1**. Have students pay special attention to the boldfaced words and underline any other unfamiliar words.

3. Have students work in pairs to complete **Exercise 2**. When done, go over the answers as a class by having volunteers give the answers. Go over any other unfamiliar words students underlined.

 Go to www.mynorthstarlab.com for additional *Background and Vocabulary* practice.

②FOCUS ON LISTENING

◖ SKILLS

Predict content; listen for main ideas; identify details; make inferences; express opinions about soccer; correct false statements.

✿✿✿ Ⓐ LISTENING ONE: The Sports File

 Go to www.mynorthstarlab.com to listen to *The Sports File*.

Suggested Time: 5 minutes

Listening One is a radio show dedicated to sports. Students listen to interviews with people from all over the world about why they like soccer. The conversational style is somewhat informal.

Have students listen to the beginning of the radio show and complete the exercise. Ask them why they chose their answers. Explain to students that their answers are just predictions. Affirm each prediction as a possibility.

LISTENING STRATEGY: Interviews

Asking questions about the topic of the listening is a good pre-listening strategy.

1. Working in a small group, students write interview questions to pose to their classmates on the topic of sports.

2. Have students break into pairs. One student will be the interviewer and the other student will be an interviewee. The interviewer will ask a question, listen, and record the answer. Then they will read what they have written to confirm the recorded response with the interviewee.

3. Tell students that in Listening One, they will be listening to an interview with soccer fans. Brainstorm a list of some of the questions that might be asked in the audio. As students listen to the recording, confirm questions asked and add others to the list.

✪✪✪ LISTEN FOR MAIN IDEAS

1. Play the entire radio show and have students complete the exercise. If necessary, play the interview again to allow students to finish.

2. Go over the answers as a class. If there is any disagreement, listen to the show again, stopping where appropriate to resolve any disagreements.

✪✪✪ LISTEN FOR DETAILS

1. Explain that students will now listen for details—specific information that supports the main ideas of the listening.

2. Divide the class into small groups and have students complete **Exercise 1**.

3. Go over the answers with the whole class. Ask individual students to read the details they completed. If there is disagreement about a detail, listen again to resolve it.

4. When done, ask students if their predictions from Section 2A were correct. If not, ask students to share what they assumed.

Expansion/Homework

Ask students to complete a full outline of the listening, including main ideas and details. Have them do this before completing the listening activities, then use the outline to complete both exercises. Then allow students to listen again to check their answers and/or fill in any gaps in the exercises.

✪✪✪ MAKE INFERENCES

1. Explain that in the following exercise students must determine the correct answers based on information from the conversation. Explain that they will not hear specific answers, but must determine the best answers based on what the speakers say.

2. Play each excerpt, stopping after each one to give students enough time to select their answer. Have students compare answers with a classmate's. Then go over the answers as a class. Encourage discussion. Continue until you have listened to all excerpts.

REACHING ALL STUDENTS: Make Inferences

- **Less Proficient:** Ask students to brainstorm groups of people such as students, grandparents, policemen, artists, and Canadians. For each group, ask student groups to infer whether the group represents people that like soccer or do not like soccer.

- **More Proficient:** Acting as a soccer fan, students respond orally to interview questions.

✪✪✪ EXPRESS OPINIONS

Suggested Time: 15 minutes

1. Tell students that it is now their turn to express their own opinions about the topic of soccer.

2. Have students look at the scale in **Exercise 1** and put an *X* that represents their opinion. Then have students write two reasons for their opinion (**Exercise 2**).

3. For **Exercise 3**, have students work in small groups to compare and discuss their opinions.

4. If time allows, bring the class back together and ask for volunteers from groups to share some of the opinions and reasons. Encourage discussion.

CRITICAL THINKING

Give students the following questions for discussion in small groups before discussing as a whole class:

1. Who does Gilberto compare to a bird?

   Answer: A soccer player jumping in the air

2. According to the text, is the USA a country that loves soccer or a country that doesn't understand?

   Answer: The United States is a country that doesn't understand.

3. What can you conclude from Gilberto's comments?

   Answer: He loves the game of soccer.

4. If you wanted to convince a friend to become a soccer fan, what would you do?

   Answer: Answers will vary, but students should support their answers.

✪✪✪ Ⓑ LISTENING TWO: America Talks

 Go to www.mynorthstarlab.com to listen to *America Talks*.

Suggested Time: 10 minutes

Listening Two is a radio call-in show where listeners call and express their opinions. Students listen to a number of callers who share their opinions about why soccer is not popular in the United States.

1. Explain that students will hear a radio call-in show where people express their views on the popularity of soccer.

2. Have students listen to the show then complete the exercise, correcting false information. Then have students compare answers. Play the audio again if there is disagreement.

3. Go over the answers with the class. Then ask students if they were surprised by what they learned.

◖ SKILLS

Organize information from the listenings in a chart; synthesize the information in a role play.

STEP 1: Organize   Suggested Time: 10 minutes

1. Point to the chart and explain that students will consider why soccer is popular in most countries and why it isn't popular in the United States.

2. Have students complete the exercise. Then go over the answers as a class.

STEP 2: Synthesize   Suggested Time: 20 minutes

1. Explain that students are going to create a role play based on the information in the chart they completed in Step 1. Tell them that they should make the conversation as natural as possible.

2. Give students a few minutes to prepare and practice their role plays. Move around the room and provide help where necessary with pronunciation and vocabulary.

3. When all students are finished, invite a few pairs to come up and act out their conversation.

Go to www.mynorthstarlab.com for *Notetaking* and *Academic Skills Practice.*

③FOCUS ON SPEAKING

A **VOCABULARY**

◖ SKILLS

Review vocabulary from Listenings One and Two; expand vocabulary by learning and using idiomatic expressions related to sports; use new vocabulary creatively in a conversation.

✿ REVIEW   Suggested Time: 10 minutes

Go to www.mynorthstarlab.com for *Review.*

1. Explain that students will read a sentence with one underlined word and then look at the words in parentheses to decide which one does not belong. Do the first item as a class. Then have students complete the exercise.

2. Call on individual students to read the answers. Encourage students to explain why the words they crossed out don't make sense in the contexts of the sentences.

⊙⊙ EXPAND

1. Have students look at the picture and describe what they see. Help with any vocabulary words students might not know by writing them on the board (construction site, project, etc.).

2. Explain that the conversation in **Exercise 1** has idioms related to sports. Remind students that idioms are expressions whose meaning can't be determined from knowing the parts.

3. Read the conversation aloud with the class and then have students read the conversation in pairs, each taking one role.

4. Have students continue to work in pairs to complete **Exercise 2**. When done, have individual students write the answers on the board. Go over the idioms for pronunciation if necessary.

Link to *NorthStar: Reading and Writing 1*
If students are also using the companion text, you might want to have them write a conversation using the sports idioms from Expand in Unit 10 of the *Reading and Writing* strand.

VOCABULARY EXPANSION: Prefixes and Suffixes

Ask students to scan the audioscript for Unit 10 to find words with prefixes and suffixes. As students volunteer words, sort them in two columns labeled *prefixes* and *suffixes*. Discuss the meaning of the words in each category. Ask students to contribute other words to add to the list. For example, *-ly—lonely, -ed—married, -s—friends, -er—teacher*. Challenge students to form new words by adding prefixes or suffixes.

⊙ CREATE

1. Ask the class to think of sports as you write them on the board. Then ask about other "sports" such as cheerleading, poker, eating contests and try to get more of these on the board. Others might include mud wrestling, car racing, and skydiving. Ask why these are not sports and allow for a brief discussion.

2. Have students work in small groups to complete **Exercise 1**. Have students practice their conversation, but not write it down.

3. When done, have several groups share their conversation with the class (**Exercise 2**). Ask other students which students they agree with in the group and why.

Go to www.mynorthstarlab.com for additional *Vocabulary* practice.

✪✪ B GRAMMAR: *Should* for Ideas and Opinions

📁 Go to www.mynorthstarlab.com for *Grammar Chart* and *Exercise 2*.

◖ SKILLS

Learn *should* for ideas and opinions; give opinions using *should*.

Suggested Time: 25 minutes

1. Read the sentences in the cartoon in **Exercise 1** with students. Then have students underline the verbs and circle the word before each verb. Have students tell you the answers.

2. Go over the chart with the class. Ask individual students to read the explanations and the examples. Assist students with any pronunciation difficulties by having the whole class repeat after you.

3. Have students complete **Exercise 2** and compare answers with a partner's when done. Then go over the answers as a class.

4. Have students work individually to complete **Exercise 3**. Then go over the answers as a class.

5. Have students write their own opinion in **Exercise 4**. Then have them work with one or two other students to share their sentences. When done, bring the class back together and ask for volunteers to read their sentences. Encourage discussion.

Expansion/Homework

(1) You might want to assign Exercises 2–4 for homework and check answers in class. (2) For further practice, offer exercises from *Focus on Grammar 1*, 2nd Edition or Azar's *Basic English Grammar*, 3rd Edition. See the Grammar Book References on page 224 of the student book for specific units and chapters.

 Go to www.mynorthstarlab.com for additional *Grammar* practice.

C SPEAKING

◖ SKILLS

Practice intonation for emphasizing important words; introduce reasons into a discussion; integrate the concepts, vocabulary, grammar, pronunciation, and function from the unit to design and present a TV ad.

✪✪ PRONUNCIATION: Stress on Important Words

Suggested Time: 25 minutes

1. Go over the information and play the example conversation. Then play the conversation again and have students repeat chorally. If necessary, explain that intonation (the ups and downs of a speaker's voice and the words he/she chooses to emphasize) can change the meaning. Intonation adds strength to a message.

2. Play the conversations in **Exercise 1** and have students repeat chorally. Then have students practice the conversations with a partner.

3. Go over the instructions for **Exercise 2** and complete the first item with the class. Stress *sports* in the first sentence and then stress *on TV* to illustrate how the exercise should be completed. Then have students work with a partner to complete the exercise. Move around the room and offer assistance if necessary.

4. Go over the instructions for **Exercise 3**. Divide the class into small groups and have students complete the exercise. Move around the room and offer assistance if necessary.

✪✪ FUNCTION: Introducing Reasons and Results

Suggested Time: 15 minutes

1. Explain to students that there are specific phrases they can use in a conversation to give a reason. Sometimes speakers want to introduce a reason that is expected, so they will use *because*. But if a reason is unexpected, they use *even though*.

2. Ask for volunteers to read the phrases in the box. Help with pronunciation as necessary. Go over pronunciation with the whole class.

3. Have students work in pairs to complete the exercise. Go over pronunciation of the sporting events as a class and then go over the example with the class. Have students work in pairs to complete the activity. Move around the room and provide assistance where necessary.

4. When complete, go around the room and have individual pairs say one event Nicole will or won't watch and why.

✪✪✪ PRODUCTION: Presentation

Suggested Time: 45–50 minutes

If you wish to assign a different speaking task than the one in this section, see page 206. The alternative topics relate to the theme of the unit, but may not target the same grammar, pronunciation, or function taught in the unit.

1. Explain that students will make a 30 second TV ad for a game that will be on TV next week. The goal is to try to convince Americans to watch the game. Go over the task box with the class.

2. Have students decide what their message or main idea is; how will they convince American's to watch? Explain that TV ads are very short so they must

have a good, strong point made quickly. Start with a class brainstorming session to help students get ideas. Some ideas are: *Are you hungry for something different? Start a new tradition. Understand the rest of the world.*

3. Give students time to think of their main idea and complete Step 1. Have students write it out as one sentence, thinking about intonation.

4. When students have a main idea, have them go over the unit and find reasons to support their message, or think of their own. Have students make notes about the reasons, but discourage writing out complete sentences or scripts.

5. For Steps 2–3, have students work in pairs to practice their ad. One student will practice while the other listens and considers the questions. Have the listener respond to all the questions, then switch roles.

6. For Step 4, have individual students perform their ads for the class. The students who are listening should answer the listening questions for all the ads. When done, take a class poll on the best ad.

Expansion/Homework
Instead of voting on the best ad, you can have students rank the ads, choosing the top five or ten.

 Link to *NorthStar: Reading and Writing 1*
Have students prepare a TV ad featuring a professional athlete giving advice to young athletes on going professional. Have the professional athlete describe his/her life, explain the pros and cons, and give advice.

✪ ALTERNATIVE SPEAKING TOPICS

These topics give students an alternative opportunity to explore and discuss issues related to the unit theme.

✪ RESEARCH TOPICS

Suggested Time: 20–30 minutes in class

1. Have students turn to page 222. Review the instructions for the activity with the class.

2. Brainstorm a list of possible questions with the class. Emphasize that it is important to ask the same questions to all people in the survey.

3. Have students survey at least five people and bring the results to class. In small groups, have students tally their results. Then have groups present their results to the class.

 Go to www.mynorthstarlab.com for *Student Speaking Models, Integrated Task, Video Activity, Internet Activity,* and *Unit 10 Achievement Test.*

Student Book Answer Key

UNIT 1

1C BACKGROUND AND VOCABULARY

3, page 5

a

4, page 5

1. f	**3.** g	**5.** h	**7.** d	**9.** b
2. e	**4.** c	**6.** a	**8.** i	

2A LISTENING ONE, page 6

1. a telephone call
2. *Answers will vary.*

LISTEN FOR MAIN IDEAS

1, page 6

1. T	**2.** F	**3.** T	**4.** F	**5.** T

LISTEN FOR DETAILS, pages 6–7

1. b	**3.** b	**5.** a	**7.** b
2. a	**4.** b	**6.** b	

MAKE INFERENCES, page 7

1. b	**2.** b	**3.** a	**4.** a

2B LISTENING TWO, page 8

1. F; *Experiment* groups always come from different cities.
2. F; Annie and her group spent 4 weeks together in Costa Rica.
3. T
4. T
5. F; Annie's Spanish name is "Ana." OR: "Ana" is not Annie's real name.
6. T
7. T
8. F; *Experiment* groups usually stay in a foreign country for three, four or five weeks.
9. F; *Experiment* groups go to 27 different countries.
10. F; Some *Experiment* students take classes in a foreign language.

STEP 1: Organize, page 9

	Friendship Force	Experiment in International Living
2.	✓	
3.		✓
4.		✓
5.	✓	
6.	✓	✓
7.		✓
8.		✓
9.	✓	✓
10.	✓	✓
11.	✓	✓

REVIEW, pages 10–11

1. international	4. stay	7. spend
2. is interested in	5. culture	8. excited about
3. traveling	6. make friends	9. application

EXPAND

2, pages 12–13

Answers will vary. Suggested answers:

Picture 2: That's Saranya. She's talkative.
Picture 3: That's James. He's lazy.
That's Kelly. She's happy.
That's Kelly and Shiro. They're hardworking
Picture 4: That's Lakesha. She's funny / happy.
Picture 5: Those are the students in my Spanish class. They're interesting / calm.

3B GRAMMAR

1, page 15

1. present forms of *be*: <u>is</u>, <u>I'm</u>, <u>isn't</u>, <u>you're</u>
past forms of *be*: was, were, were
2. negative form of *be*: isn't

2, page 17

2.	aren't / 're not	9.	wasn't
3.	Is	10.	was
4.	isn't / 's not	11.	aren't / 're not
5.	isn't	12.	'm not
6.	are / 're	13.	isn't / 's not
7.	is	14.	are
8.	was	15.	is

PRONUNCIATION

4, page 19

   a. I'm from Tokyo. How about you?

   d. Yes, I am. How about you?

   c. What's your major?

UNIT 2

1C BACKGROUND AND VOCABULARY

2, page 25

1. c	3. f	5. h	7. i	9. b
2. d	4. g	6. e	8. a	

2A LISTENING ONE, page 26

1. Eco-fashion is fashion that uses organic materials like wool and cotton.
2. Eco-fashion is good for the environment.
3. *Answers will vary.*

LISTEN FOR MAIN IDEAS, page 27

2, 3, 5

LISTEN FOR DETAILS, page 27

1. b	3. a	5. b	7. a
2. b	4. b	6. b	

MAKE INFERENCES, page 28

1. a 2. c 3. c

2B LISTENING TWO, pages 29–30

1. b 2. a 3. b 4. a 5. b 6. b

STEP 1: Organize, page 31

	Fashion Designers	Gee's Bend Women
What do they do?	Makes trendy clothes with unusual materials; makes eco-fashion	Make quilts from old clothing; remember loved ones
Why do they use recycled materials?	They're beautiful and it's good for the environment.	Old materials don't cost any money.
Where do they live?	All over the world	Alabama

REVIEW, pages 32–33

1. advice	4. unusual	7. environment
2. recycled	5. trendy	8. famous
3. material	6. trash	

EXPAND

2, page 34

1. c	3. a	5. f	7. e
2. d	4. b	6. g	

3B GRAMMAR

1–2, page 4

verbs: is becoming, are selling, 's wearing, is wearing

be + verb + *-ing*

be is before the subject

4, pages 35–36

2. 'm watching		5. 's making
3. 's making		6. 's wearing
4. is; using		7. are becoming

PRONUNCIATION

1, page 37

jacket: 2	quilt: 1
shirt: 1	wedding: 2

2, page 37

ga rage	rea son	de cide
trash	a gree	po cket
clothes	fa mous	mo ther
po pu lar	ex pen sive	stu dent
jeans	bro ther	re cy cle
fa shion	belt	

3a, pages 37–38

2. listen, music	9. advice
3. answer, question	10. believe
4. pocket	11. designs
5. garage	12. invite, students
6. decide	13. visit, parents
7. agree	14. study, fashion
8. sister	

3b, page 38

1. music, question, pocket, garage, sister, advice, students, parents, fashion
2. listen, answer, agree, believe, designs, invite, visit, study
3. **a.** Most **b.** Most

4, page 38

A: What's in the box? Is that a wool <u>coat</u>?

B: Let's see . . . There's a <u>blanket</u>, some <u>kitchen</u> things, and . . . what's this?

A: A <u>shirt</u>? Maybe a <u>jacket</u>? I can't <u>decide</u>.

B: Let's keep it. The <u>color</u> is nice.

UNIT 3

1A PREDICT

1, page 45

1. DJ
2. record / LP
3. turntable
4. mike (microphone)
5. rapper

2, page 45

1. b   2. c

1C BACKGROUND AND VOCABULARY

2, page 48

vinyl records (LPs); drum machines

3, page 48

1. in the 70s
2. rhythm
3. slang
4. just
5. played
6. rhymed
7. poor
8. neighborhoods
9. great
10. melody
11. musical instruments
12. popular

2A LISTENING ONE, page 49

1. b
2. b
3. *Answers will vary.*

LISTEN FOR MAIN IDEAS

1, page 49

1. F; King Kool was a rapper in the 70s.
2. T
3. T
4. T
5. T
6. F; Tupac wrote songs because he was angry.
7. T
8. F; Young African Americans understood Tupac's songs.
9. F; Tupac's music is still popular today.

LISTEN FOR DETAILS, page 50

1. a   3. a   5. a
2. a   4. b   6. b

MAKE INFERENCES, page 50

1. b, d   3. b, d   5. a, c
2. b, d   4. a, d

2B LISTENING TWO, page 51

1. c   3. d   5. a   7. e
2. f   4. b   6. g

STEP 1: Organize, page 52

Answers will vary. Suggested answers:

Positive	Negative
1. **The songs tell people ...** about real things. about rappers' lives.	1. **The songs tell people about bad things, such as ...** guns, drugs and sex.
2. **The rhythm is ...** great.	2. **Rap isn't real music because ...** the songs have no melody. the rappers don't play any musical instruments.
3. **People can learn about ...** what's happening in the U.S. cities.	3. **The words in rap songs are ...** slang. bad words.

REVIEW, page 53

Conversation 1: "I don't like rap."

A: 1. Do you like rap music?

B: 2. No, I don't think rap is really music.

A: 3. I agree. Rappers are not real musicians.

B: 4. You're right. They don't sing or play any musical instruments.

A: 5. That's true. And the songs are just slang words that rhyme.

B: 6. And the words are so bad! I don't understand why rap is so popular.

A: 7. I don't understand it either!

B: 8. I guess different people like different types of music.

Conversation 2: "Do you like Brazilian jazz?"

B: 1. Did you ever hear Brazilian jazz?

A: 2. Yeah, I love Brazilian jazz! It has great rhythm.

B: 3. I know! I just bought an old CD by Tom Jobim.

A: 4. The cool Brazilian singer? When did it come out?

B: 5. In the 80s, I think.

A: 6. That's old. Where did you buy it?

B: 7. At a great music store in my neighborhood.

A: 8. I want to buy some jazz CDs. Let's go there now!

EXPAND

1, page 54

5: I love it.   It's my favorite (kind of music).

4: I like it very much.   I like it a lot.

3: I like it.

2: I can take it or leave it.   (It's OK, but) I'm not crazy about it.

1: I don't like it (at all).

0: I hate it.

3B GRAMMAR

1, page 55

1. means, speak, don't play, know, is, love
2. means, know, is, love

2, page 56

Non-Action (Stative) Verbs				Action Verbs
Situation	Idea	Feeling	Sense	
means	know	love	hear	play
is	understand	like		happens
have	believe	want		sing
	think			listen

3, page 57

2. I am
3. do you know
4. is
5. hear
6. are listening
7. know
8. Do you see
9. They're looking
10. think
11. am turning
12. need
13. is
14. don't hear
15. don't really understand
16. know
17. mean
18. want
19. understand
20. hates

PRONUNCIATION

2, page 59

1. a   2. a   3. b   4. a   5. b

UNIT 4

1A PREDICT, page 65

1. necklace
2. earrings
3. ring
4. bracelet

1C BACKGROUND AND VOCABULARY, pages 67–68

a. steal
b. wealthy
c. appear
d. valuable
e. advertises
f. weigh more
g. traditions
h. huge
i. luck
j. history
k. are worth

2A LISTENING ONE, page 68

1. Yes   2. Yes   3. No

LISTEN FOR MAIN IDEAS, page 69

Order: 1, 3, 2

LISTEN FOR DETAILS, page 69

1. b   2. b   3. a   4. b   5. a   6. a

MAKE INFERENCES, page 70

1. b   2. b   3. b

2B LISTENING TWO

2, page 70

1. color
2. Cut
3. Carat
4. clarity

STEP 1: Organize, page 71

	Cut	Color	Clarity	Carat
1. Why did King Louis XIV of France want to buy the Hope Diamond?				✓
2. Why is the Hope Diamond so valuable today?	✓	✓	✓	✓
3. What does an excellent diamond have?			✓	
4. What don't most valuable diamonds have?		✓		

REVIEW, page 72

1. worth
2. valuable
3. huge
4. carats
5. sparkles
6. history
7. fascinating
8. steals
9. wealthy

EXPAND, page 73

1. d   2. e   3. b   4. f   5. a   6. c

3B GRAMMAR

1, page 74

1. sparkles, weighs
2. d. doesn't mean, e. don't cost
3. g

2, pages 75–76

2. see
3. read
4. don't know
5. use
6. becomes
7. wears
8. opens
9. wears
10. Do; see
11. weighs
12. sparkles
13. comes
14. brings
15. wear
16. do; believe
17. sounds
18. brings
19. have

PRONUNCIATION

3, pages 77–78

1. s	4. s, s
2. z, z, z	5. z, əz
3. s, z, əz	

UNIT 5

1C BACKGROUND AND VOCABULARY

2, page 85

b

3, page 86

1. b	4. a	7. a
2. a	5. a	8. a
3. b	6. b	9. a

2A LISTENING ONE, page 87

1. No	3. Yes	5. No	7. No
2. No	4. Yes	6. Yes	8. Yes

LISTEN FOR MAIN IDEAS

1, pages 87–88

1. T
2. F; The group members write about their memories.
3. T
4. T
5. T
6. T
7. F; The members are always happy to get together.

LISTEN FOR DETAILS, page 88

1. b	2. a	3. b	4. c	5. c	6. b

MAKE INFERENCES, page 89

1. a	2. b	3. b	4. a

2B LISTENING TWO, page 90

1. memory	3. name	5. words
2. clouds	4. fish	6. finished

STEP 1: Organize

2, page 91

People with Alzheimer's Disease Lost:	People in the Writers' Group Found:
their cars	a new hobby
their old life	something they can do well
their independence	a place to talk about their feelings
their jobs	people who understand them
their old friends	

REVIEW, pages 92–93

1. **A:** My grandmother has Alzheimer's disease.
   B: I'm sorry to hear that. It's a terrible illness.

2. **A:** All of our relatives are helping her.
   B: That's great. But your family may need some support, too.

3. **A:** Sometimes she can't remember our names.
   B: Yes, people with Alzheimer's often forget names, even the names of their family members.

4. **A:** She looks so lonely sometimes.
   B: Maybe she can join a support group. Then she can make some new friends.

5. **B:** When Elsa got Alzheimer's disease, she couldn't keep her job as a nurse.
   A: I know. She was so sad to lose her job. She really loved it.

6. **B:** Elsa can't remember things that happened yesterday or last week.
   A: That's true. But she has some clear memories of her childhood. She wrote a story about a day when she got lost in a park.

7. **B:** Elsa joined a support group, and she made friends with the other members.
   A: Yes. And then she didn't feel so lonely.

8. **B:** A psychologist helps the members of Elsa's support group.
   A: Yes, but the members all help each other, too.

3B GRAMMAR, page 95

1. **B:** What does Herb need to do?
   A: Herb needs to choose Rhoda's clothes.

2. **B:** Why doesn't Sarah want to join the writers' group?
   A: Sarah doesn't want to join the writers' group because she has Alzheimer's.

3. **B:** Why does Joe like to go to the writers' group?
   A: Joe likes to go to the writers' group because he has fun there.

4. **B:** What does Elsa like to do?
   A: Elsa likes to help the other members with their stories.

5. **B:** Why does Sarah want to make new friends?
   A: Sarah wants to make new friends because she feels lonely. / she doesn't get together with her old friends anymore.

6. **B:** Why do people need to go to the Alzheimer's Organization?
   A: People need to go to the Alzheimer's Organization because they can learn how to help their relatives.

PRONUNCIATION

1, page 96

different

3c, pages 96–97

1. /ɛ/, /ey/
2. /ey/, /ey/, /ey/
3. /ɛ/
4. /ɛ/
5. /ɛ/, /ɛ/, /ey/
6. /ey/, /ɛ/
7. /ey/
8. /ey/
9. /ɛ/

4, pages 97–98

1. take a break
2. Go ahead.
3. get lost
4. make friends
5. made a mistake
6. get together

UNIT 6

1C BACKGROUND AND VOCABULARY

2, page 103

b, c, e

3, pages 103–104

1. have a company
2. makes a lot of money
3. are new and different
4. worked at a job
5. you make an effort to do it
6. something is difficult or different
7. the wrong way
8. are a lot of fun

2A LISTENING ONE, pages 104–105

1. a   2. b   3. b

LISTEN FOR MAIN IDEAS

1, page 105

1. F; K-K started her business when she was 10 years old.
2. F; Wristies keep your hands and wrists warm. Or: Wristies don't keep your fingers warm.
3. F; K-K's mother didn't help her make the first pair of Wristies. Or: K-K made the first pair of Wristies by herself.
4. T
5. T

LISTEN FOR DETAILS, page 106

2. a   4. c   6. c   8. c
3. b   5. b   7. b

MAKE INFERENCES, page 107

1. b   2. c   3. a

2B LISTENING TWO

1, page 108

1. T
2. F; K-K listened to her mother, her friends, and many other people.
3. T
4. F; Adults don't think it's OK to make mistakes.
5. T
6. T
7. F; The students in Professor Ray's class will try to meditate.
8. F; The students will remember a time when they were not afraid.

STEP 1: Organize, page 109

2. 1, 2   3. 2   4. 3   5. 2   6. 3

REVIEW, page 111

1. afraid
2. made mistakes
3. creative
4. owner
5. successful
6. try
7. exciting
8. experience

EXPAND

2, pages 112–113

1. b   3. a   5. g   7. h
2. d   4. c   6. e   8. f

3B GRAMMAR

1, page 113

b. about the present: Are there, there are
   about the past: Were there, there were, there weren't, There was
   singular: There was

2, pages 114–115

1. there aren't
2. There was
3. there aren't
4. Was there
5. There are
6. there are
7. there isn't
8. There is
9. There is
10. There were
11. there are

PRONUNCIATION, page 116

There are 7 words with *th*:

333,333 = <u>th</u>ree hundred <u>th</u>irty <u>th</u>ree <u>th</u>ousand, <u>th</u>ree hundred <u>th</u>irty <u>th</u>ree

1, page 116

1. They're; with
2. There's; the; thumb.
3. them; others; them
4. They; them
5. then; thought; these; things
6. mother; anything
7. them; there's

2, page 117

1. thinks   3. anything   5. thumb
2. mother   4. thought

UNIT 7

1A PREDICT, page 123

1. field   5. leaves   9. seedling
2. river   6. branch   10. soil
3. wood   7. trunk
4. seeds   8. roots

1C BACKGROUND AND VOCABULARY

2, pages 126–127

2. a   4. a   6. b   8. a   10. a
3. b   5. b   7. a   9. b

2A LISTENING ONE, page 128

1. b
2. *Answers will vary.*

LISTEN FOR MAIN IDEAS, pages 128–129

Part One: 4, 1, 3, 2
Part Two: 8, 6, 5, 7
Part Three: 10, 9, 11

LISTEN FOR DETAILS, page 129

1. a   3. b   5. b   7. b
2. a   4. a   6. a   8. a

MAKE INFERENCES, page 130

1. b   2. b   3. b   4. a

2B LISTENING TWO

1, page 131

1. F; Most Mayan people in Guatemala don't have equal rights.
2. T
3. F; Rigoberta was the first native person to win the Nobel Peace Prize.
4. F; Rigoberta stopped going to school when she was eight.

5. F; Guatemala didn't have a democratic government at that time.
6. T
7. T
8. F; Rigoberta said that war is not necessary.
9. F; Rigoberta lives a non-violent life.

STEP 1: Organize

1, page 132

	Wangari	Rigoberta	Both
1.			✓
2.			✓
3.		✓	
4.	✓		
5.		✓	
6.			✓
7.		✓	
8.	✓		

REVIEW, page 133

1b. encouraged   5b. without
2b. destroy   6b. violence
3b. beat her up   7b. democracy
4b. jail   8b. political

EXPAND, page 134

2. were against   4. spoke out   6. fighting for
3. care about   5. had courage

3B GRAMMAR

1, pages 135–136

Verbs that tell about the past:

was	decided	continued
started	flew	laughed at
said	picked	Did you put out
waited	returned	asked
saw	did not put out	answered

1.
   b. started   **g.** continued
   c. waited   **h.** laughed
   d. decided   **i.** asked
   e. picked   **j.** answered
   f. returned

2.
   a. was   **d.** flew
   b. said   **e.** put
   c. saw

3. did not put out
4. Did you put out the fire?

2, pages 138–139

2.	picked	18.	didn't want
3.	was	19.	was
4.	did	20.	had
5.	didn't dream	21.	wanted
6.	did she do	22.	did she speak out
7.	worked	23.	believed
8.	went	24.	had
9.	made	25.	cared about
10.	stayed	26.	traveled
11.	took care of	27.	did Eleanor do
12.	did	28.	died
13.	loved	29.	didn't stop
14.	listened	30.	began
15.	happened	31.	helped
16.	became	32.	fought for
17.	decided		

PRONUNCIATION

1, page 140

1.	/ɪd/	4.	/t/	7.	/ɪd/
2.	/d/	5.	/ɪd/	8.	/d/
3.	/t/	6.	/d/	9.	/t/

2, pages 140–141

3; After her parents died, Eleanor <u>lived</u> /d/ with her aunt.

8; Her lessons <u>helped</u> /t/ Eleanor many times later in her life.

7; Eleanor always <u>remembered</u> /d/ Marie Souvestre's lessons.

1; Eleanor Roosevelt had a sad childhood.

5; Eleanor <u>loved</u> /d/ her school and her teacher, Marie Souvestre.

6; Marie Souvestre <u>wanted</u> /ɪd/ her students to be strong and independent.

2; Both of her parents <u>died</u> /d/ when she was very young.

4; Then her aunt <u>decided</u> /ɪd/ to send her to a girls' school in England.

3, page 141

a. Rigoberta Menchu didn't finish elementary school.
b. She stopped going to school to help her family.
c. She continued to study on her own, after work.
d. Rigoberta joined a political group when she was a teenager.
e. She wanted to help poor workers.
f. The government decided to destroy the political group.
g. The government killed everyone in Rigoberta's family.
h. Rigoberta left Guatemala.
i. She went to Mexico.
j. She worked with other Guatemalans to bring democracy to Guatemala.
k. Rigoberta helped many people.
l. She won the Nobel Peace Prize for her work.

UNIT 8

1B SHARE INFORMATION

1, page 148

1.	signal	3.	honk	5.	lane
2.	pay attention	4.	tailgate		

2, page 148

3, 4, 1, 2

1C BACKGROUND AND VOCABULARY

2, page 149

c

3, pages 149–150

1.	a	3.	a	5.	b	7.	a
2.	a	4.	b	6.	a	8.	a

LISTEN FOR MAIN IDEAS, page 151

1.	Marie	3.	John	5.	John
2.	John	4.	Marie	6.	Marie

LISTEN FOR DETAILS, page 151

1.	F	3.	T	5.	F	7.	T	9.	F
2.	T	4.	F	6.	T	8.	F	10.	F

MAKE INFERENCES, page 152

1.	c	2.	a	3.	b	4.	b	5.	a	6.	a

2B LISTENING TWO, pages 153–154

1.	b	2.	b	3.	b	4.	a	5.	b

STEP I: Organize, page 154

Answers will vary. Suggested answers:

	Driving Problems	Where They Got Help	What They Learned
John	1. driving while tired 2. changing lanes without using his signal	traffic school	• Don't drive when you're tired. • Don't forget to signal. • It's dangerous.
Marie	1. getting angry 2. tailgating 3. honking	traffic school	You can't control other drivers. You can only control yourself.
Allen	1. afraid to cross bridge 2. afraid a truck will hit him 3. afraid of falling into water	psychologist	• Think about other things you can do well. • Look straight ahead while you're driving.

REVIEW

1, pages 156–157

1. crowded
2. rude
3. control
4. phobias
5. intersection
6. injured
7. anonymous
8. traffic school

EXPAND, page 158

1. b　2. a　3. b　4. a　5. b　6. a

3B GRAMMAR

1, page 159

a. was driving, forgot, got, was driving

b. similar: tell about the past

different: *Was driving* is the past progressive, and *forgot* and *got* are the simple past.

2, pages 160–161

1. studied
2. learned
3. were
4. were driving
5. got
6. tailgated
7. traveled
8. was
9. rode
10. felt
11. was riding
12. honked
13. was driving
14. visited
15. injured
16. were fighting

PRONUNCIATION, page 162

The driver on my left / turned into my lane / without signaling / I tried to stop / but I couldn't / I hit him.

UNIT 9

IC BACKGROUND AND VOCABULARY

1, page 172

1. especially
2. siblings
3. aren't busy
4. enough
5. hard
6. raise
7. have
8. get married
9. make . . . money
10. can't afford

2A LISTENING ONE, page 173

1. a
2. *Answers will vary.*

LISTEN FOR MAIN IDEAS

1, page 174

1. lonely
2. hard
3. a happy child
4. a good life
5. busy

LISTEN FOR DETAILS, page 174

1. F; Marion had a baby when she was 38.
2. F; Marion and Mark can take care of Tonia.
3. T
4. F; Maria read that many only children are more popular *than* children with siblings.
5. T
6. T
7. F; Jay is never lonely.

MAKE INFERENCES, page 175

1. a　2. a　3. b

2B LISTENING TWO, pages 175–176

1. c　3. b　5. c　7. a
2. a　4. b　6. b　8. b

STEP 1: Organize, pages 176–177

Answers may vary. Suggested answers:

Advantages	Disadvantages
1. It's easier for older parents to raise just one child.	1. It's a hard decision if you love children.
2. Parents can spend more time with their child.	2. Some only children want to play with other children, not with adults.
3. Only children are often more popular than children with siblings.	3. When the parents are busy, only children have no one to play with at home.
4. Only children are more independent than children with siblings.	4. Some only children feel lonely.
5. Some only children feel special.	5. Some only children feel different from their friends.
6. It's less expensive to raise just one child. Parents can give their only child a good life.	

REVIEW, pages 178–179

1. raise
2. busy
3. tired
4. took care of
5. especially
6. have
7. got married
8. hard
9. can't afford
10. make; money

EXPAND

2 and 3, pages 180–181

This is what THEY say:	Our responses:
"Problem" #1: When children are selfish, _c_	_2_ …They are more independent than children with siblings. This means _b_
"Problem" #2: When children are spoiled, _f_	_3_ …They have many close friends. This means _a_
"Problem" #3: When children don't get along well with others, _e_	_1_ …Our children are usually self-confident, not self-centered. This means _d_

3B GRAMMAR

1, page 182

1. three parts
2. be
3. going to; It doesn't change.
4. the base form of the verb

2, page 183

1. Are; going to
2. 'm /am going to
3. aren't going to
4. 're /are going to
5. 'm / am going to
6. 'm / am going to
7. 're / are going to

PRONUNCIATION, page 184

A: going to
B: gonna

1, pages 184–185

1. a   2. b   3. b   4. a   5. b

UNIT 10

1A PREDICT, page 191

1. a   2. b   3. *Answers will vary.*

1C BACKGROUND AND VOCABULARY

2, page 193

1. things
2. watch
3. play sports
4. get points
5. game
6. are from
7. the numbers that show who is winning a game
8. play
9. everyone in the world can understand it

LISTEN FOR MAIN IDEAS, page 194

1. c   2. a

LISTEN FOR DETAILS, pages 194–195

1. a, c   2. a, c   3. b, c   4. a, d

MAKE INFERENCES, pages 195–196

1. b   2. a   3. b

2B LISTENING TWO, page 196

1. F; People call *America Talks* from all over the country.
2. T
3. F; Steve thinks sports fans in the U.S. don't need a new sport.
4. F; Drew says Pele played soccer in the U.S.
5. T

STEP 1: Organize, page 197

Why soccer is popular in most countries: 1, 2, 4, 8
Why soccer is not popular in the U.S.: 3, 5, 6, 7, 9

REVIEW, page 198

1. a car
2. "Ball"
3. take it
4. study
5. Parisian
6. almost finished
7. He is angry.
8. you can't watch those games
9. television
10. New York, Chicago, and Detroit

EXPAND

2, page 200

1. team player
2. calls the shots
3. keep the ball rolling
4. keep (your) eye on the ball
5. dropped the ball

3B GRAMMAR

1, page 200

Underlined verbs: stay, join, be, have
Circled words: should, shouldn't

2, page 201

1. should	3. should	5. should
2. should	4. shouldn't	6. shouldn't

3, page 201

1. Good sports should not / shouldn't have lots of rules.
2. Players should make a lot of money.
3. TV sports should not / shouldn't have advertisements.
4. Players should be strong.

PRONUNCIATION

2, page 203

The boldfaced words should be stressed:

1. a. I don't really like watching **sports** on TV.
   b. I don't really like watching sports on **TV**.
2. a. **All** kids should learn to play sports.
   b. All kids **should** learns to play sports.
3. a. Zizou got kicked out of the **World Cup final**.
   b. **Zizou** got kicked out of the World Cup final.
4. a. Players usually play for their home countries in the **World Cup**.
   b. Players usually play for their **home countries** in the World Cup.

Unit Word List

The **Unit Word List** is a summary of key vocabulary from the student book. The words are presented by unit, in alphabetical order.

UNIT 1

application
be excited about
be interested in
boring
calm
culture
friendly
funny
happy
hardworking
interesting
international

lazy
make friends
nervous
quiet
sad
serious
shy
spend
stay (verb)
talkative
travel (verb)

UNIT 2

advice
be dressed up
(it) doesn't fit
environment
famous
(it) fits (you) perfectly
(it) looks great on you
materials
organic
quilt

recycle (verb)
recycled (adjective)
return (something) for a
  refund
trash
trendy
try (it / them) on
unusual
wear a (small, medium,
  large)

UNIT 3

DJ
great
I can take it or leave it.
I don't like it (at all).
I hate it.
I like it.
I like it a lot.
I like it very much.
I love it.
in the 70s
It's my favorite (kind of
  music).
(It's OK, but) I'm not
  crazy about it.

just
melody
mike (microphone)
musical instruments
neighborhood
play (verb)
poor
popular
rapper
record (LP)
rhyme
rhythm
slang
turntable

UNIT 4

a lucky find
advertise
appear
be worth
bracelet
carat
clarity
color
cut
do the right thing
earring
fascinating
fortune
heartless

history
huge
luck
necklace
ring
selfish
sparkle (verb)
steal
tough luck
tradition
valuable
wealthy
weigh

UNIT 5

alone
by myself
cloud (noun)
disease
each other
finish
fish
forget
get lost
get together
hang out with
I (don't) have a good
  time when . . .
I (don't) have fun
  when . . .

I (don't) enjoy myself
  when . . .
I (don't) like to . . .
join
lonely
lose
mackerel sky
members
memory
name (noun)
on my own
relatives
remember
word

UNIT 6

be afraid
come up with
creativity
employee
exciting
feature (noun)
fingers
get around
hand
increase
make mistakes

make (someone) feel
  (+ adj.)
owner
perk
save time
successful
thumb
try
work experience
wrist

UNIT 7

be against
beat (someone) up
branch
care about
democracy
destroy
dream of
encourage
environment
field
fight for
have courage
jail
land (noun)

leaves
political (power)
river
roots
seedling
seeds
shocked
soil
speak out
take care of
trunk
violence
without
wood

UNIT 8

anonymous
complain (verb)
control
crowded
frustrated
give (someone) a break
honk
injured
intersection
lane
officer

pay attention
phobia
polite
psychologist
refuse
road rage
rude
signal (verb)
tailgate
ticket
traffic school

UNIT 9

busy
can('t) afford
close friends
enough
especially
(don't) get along well
  with others
get married
hard
have a baby / a child

independent
make (a lot of) money
raise (a child)
self-confident
selfish
siblings
spoiled
take care of
tired

UNIT 10

call the shots
drop the ball
equipment
fans
field
goal
keep (my) eye on the
  ball
keep the ball rolling

match (noun)
nationality
rule (noun)
score (noun)
team
team player
tie scores / ties
universal

Achievement Tests
Unit 1

Name: _____

Date: _____

PART 1: LISTENING

1.1 *CD 7* *Listen to the passage about Don. Check (✔) the best prediction of what the listening is about. There is only one right answer.*

_____ **A.** Don's first year of college

_____ **B.** Don's trip to Germany

_____ **C.** Don's life in New York

_____ **D.** Don's plans after college

1.2 *CD 7* *Now listen to the entire passage. Use the information to complete the sentences. Check (✔) the answers.*

1. The director wants Don to talk about _____.

_____ **A.** studying abroad

_____ **B.** filling out an application

_____ **C.** living with other people

_____ **D.** learning a language

2. During his trip, Don's German _____.

_____ **A.** got much worse

_____ **B.** improved a little

_____ **C.** improved a lot

_____ **D.** stayed the same

3. Don travelled to the Czech Republic, Belgium, and _____.

_____ **A.** England

_____ **B.** France

_____ **C.** Italy

_____ **D.** Spain

(continued on next page)

4. The students are probably interested in _____.

_____ **A.** going to college

_____ **B.** learning German

_____ **C.** making German friends

_____ **D.** studying abroad

5. Don is a _____ at Boston University.

_____ **A.** freshman

_____ **B.** sophomore

_____ **C.** junior

_____ **D.** senior

6. In Germany, Don lived with a _____.

_____ **A.** friend

_____ **B.** family

_____ **C.** relative

_____ **D.** student

1.3 🎵 *Listen to an excerpt from "The Best Summer of My Life!" from* NorthStar: *Listening and Speaking 1, Unit 1. Decide if the sentences describe Annie, Don, or both. Write the letter of the sentence in the box. One answer is already given.*

A. This person's host family spoke English.

B. Language is not so important.

C. ~~This person spent one year in another country.~~

D. This person went to Asia.

E. This person was working abroad.

F. This person lived close to the university.

Annie	Don	Both
1.	*C* **2.**	3.

PART 2: VOCABULARY

2.1   *Read the conversation. Use the words from the box to fill in the blanks. Not all the words and phrases will be used.*

application	family	international	spend
culture	happy	lazy	stay
excited about	interested in	make	travelled

ASSISTANT: How can I help you today?

STUDENT: Well, I'm _____ getting the _____ for
                 1.   **2.**
           studying abroad.

ASSISTANT: You've come to the right place. I'd like to ask you some questions.

STUDENT: Okay. I can _____ for a minute, but I have class soon.
                           3.

ASSISTANT: I understand. So, have you ever _____ to another
                                             4.
           country?

STUDENT: No. I was _____ about going abroad before.
                          5.

ASSISTANT: Do you want to _____ friends during this trip?
                              6.

STUDENT: Yeah! I love to talk with people.

ASSISTANT: Great! Well, we have some _____ programs to
                                        7.
           Europe and China. Do you want to _____ six
                                              8.
           months or a year abroad?

STUDENT: I'd love to visit China for a year. I want to learn more about the

           _____.
              9.

ASSISTANT: You seem very excited about China, so let's start there.

STUDENT: I'm so _____!
                     10.

PART 3: SKILLS FOR SPEAKING

3.1 *Complete the sentences from Don's talk. Fill in the blanks using simple present or simple past forms of* **be**. *One answer is already given.*

Good morning, everyone. This _____is_____ Don.

1. He _____ here to tell you about his study abroad experience.

2. Hello, I _____ twenty years old.

3. I am glad you _____ interested in studying abroad.

4. At first, it _____ hard for me.

5. But I _____ so excited about studying abroad.

3.2 🅲🅳7 ⑤ *Listen to the sentences. Check (✔) the rhythm of the sentence. One answer is already given.*

    ✓ **A.** DA da

    ____ **B.** da DA

    ____ **C.** da da

    ____ **D.** DA DA

1. ____ **A.** DA da DA

    ____ **B.** DA da da

    ____ **C.** da DA DA

    ____ **D.** da da DA

2. ____ **A.** da da da DA da DA

    ____ **B.** DA da da da da da

    ____ **C.** da DA da da da da

    ____ **D.** da da da da DA DA

3. ____ **A.** da da da da DA

    ____ **B.** da DA da da DA

    ____ **C.** da da DA DA da

    ____ **D.** DA da da DA da

3.3   *Read the conversation. Circle the parts where someone is asking for more information. One answer is already given.*

STUDENT 1: I have a question. (Why did you go to Germany?)

DON: I wanted to improve my German and learn more about the

culture of Germany.

STUDENT 2: Where did you live?

DON: I stayed with a wonderful host family.

STUDENT 1: Did you have problems speaking with them?

PART 4: SPEAKING

4.1   *Use one of the phrases below to ask Don from Part 1.2 for more information about Germany. You may listen again to Part 1.2.*

I have a question about . . .

Can you tell me about . . . ?

Can you explain why . . . ?

4.2   *Say two adjectives from the box that describe Don.*

boring	happy	lazy	shy
friendly	hardworking	sad	talkative

4.3 *Introducing a Classmate*

Speak for 1–2 minutes. Introduce Don to a classmate.

- Include information about Don from the listening (e.g., age, school, languages spoken).
- Use adjectives that describe personalities.
- Emphasize certain words to make the most important information clear.
- Tell students to ask you for more information when you are finished.
- Use the vocabulary and grammar from Unit 1.

Unit 1 Vocabulary Words					
culture	friendly	happy	international	spend	travel
excited about	friends	interested in	make	stay	

Unit 1 Grammar: Simple Present and Simple Past of *Be*
[simple present] • He *is* a talkative person. [simple past] • She *was* in the summer program.

Achievement Tests
Unit 2

Name: _____

Date: _____

PART 1: LISTENING

1.1 CD 1 **6** *Listen to the conversation between Dawn and Paula. Check (✔) the best prediction of what the listening is about. There is only one right answer.*

_____ **A.** buying used clothes

_____ **B.** looking at purses

_____ **C.** making old shirts

_____ **D.** recycling used clothes

1.2 CD 1 **7** *Now listen to the entire passage. Use the information to complete the sentences. Check (✔) the answers.*

1. Recycled clothing is made from _____ materials.

_____ **A.** new

_____ **B.** old

_____ **C.** unusual

_____ **D.** inorganic

2. People go to thrift stores to buy _____ clothes.

_____ **A.** new

_____ **B.** used

_____ **C.** trendy

_____ **D.** recycled

3. Paula says that her birthday is next month because she wants to

_____.

_____ **A.** help make a quilt

_____ **B.** dress like Angelina Jolie

_____ **C.** donate things to the thrift store

_____ **D.** get recycled clothes

1.3 *Check (✔) three more clothing items made from recycled materials. Use the information from the listening.*

    <u> ✓ </u>   purses

    _____ **1.** shoes

    _____ **2.** skirts

    _____ **3.** hats

    _____ **4.** dresses

    _____ **5.** gloves

1.4 CD 8 *Listen to an excerpt from "Eco-Fashion" from* NorthStar: Listening and Speaking 1, *Unit 2. Decide if the phrases describe Deborah Lindquist or Dawn. Write the letter of the phrase in the box. One answer is already given.*

    A. shirts and jeans

    B. a few years old

    C. bags and a quilt

    ~~**D.** kimonos and saris~~

    E. from the 1840s

    F. from the 1940s

	Deborah Lindquist	**Dawn**
What clothes did they recycle?	D	**2.**
How old are the materials they use?	**1.**	**3.**

PART 2: VOCABULARY

2.1 *Read the paragraph. Use the words from the box to fill in the blanks. Not all the words and phrases will be used.*

advice	famous	materials	recycled	trend
environment	fashion	organic	trash	unusual

Buying recycled clothes is a good thing to do. People can use old

_____ to make recycled clothes. Now people don't have to
        1.

throw their old clothes into the _____. Recycling is very good
                                        2.

for our _____. Recycled clothing might seem
            3.

_____ for some people, but it is very common. Even
        4.

_____ actors wear recycled clothes.
        5.

2.2 *Read the conversation. Write the letter of the phrase closest in meaning to the phrase in parentheses. Not all the phrases will be used.*

    A. wear a small

    B. didn't fit

    C. dressed up

    D. tried it on

    E. returned it for a refund

    F. fits you perfectly

    G. looks great on you

ANNIE: Wow! You're really _____ today.
                            1. (wearing special clothes)

BARBARA: Did you see my new skirt and shoes? They are made of recycled

    clothing.

ANNIE: Really? That skirt _____.
                            2. (is exactly your size)

BARBARA: At first, I bought a shirt but it _____. I
                                            3. (was the wrong size)

_____.
4. (my size is small)

ANNIE: So, what did you do?

BARBARA: I _____.
                5. (got my money back)

ANNIE: Where is this store? I want to go shopping now!

PART 3: SKILLS FOR SPEAKING

3.1 *Fill in the blanks using the present progressive form of the verbs in parentheses. One answer is already given.*

Today, we _____<u>are talking</u>_____ with Deborah Lindquist.
            (be / talk)

1. Hi there! I can see that you _____ at my purse.
                                    (be / look)

2. Now I _____ to the thrift store to buy clothes.
          (be / go)

3. My friend _____ recycled clothes today.
              (be / wear)

4. Right now I _____ a purse from old shirts and blankets.
                (be / make)

3.2 CD / Listen to the words. Write the number of syllables of each word. One answer
      9 *is already given.*

trash: __1__ syllable(s)

1. advice: _____ syllable(s)

2. medium: _____ syllable(s)

3. recycle: _____ syllable(s)

4. return: _____ syllable(s)

3.3 *Read the conversation. Circle the parts where someone is checking for understanding. One answer is already given.*

ANNIE: Meet me at the thrift store right next to the bank. (OK?)

BARBARA: Where?

ANNIE: Just take a left at the park. Got it?

BARBARA: Not really. What park are you talking about?

ANNIE: Forget it. Meet me at the bank. Any questions?

BARBARA: No. That sounds good!

PART 4: SPEAKING

4.1 *Say one expression that Dawn from Part 1.2 used to see if Paula understood her. You may listen again to Part 1.2.*

4.2 *Explain what it means to say "You're so dressed up!"*

4.3 *Agree or Disagree?*

Speak for 1–2 minutes. Say if you agree or disagree with the statement:

"More people should buy used clothes."

- Include information from the listenings.
- Use expressions for checking for understanding.
- Use the vocabulary and grammar from Unit 2.

Unit 2 Vocabulary Words				
advice dressed up	doesn't fit environment	famous looks great on you	material recycle	trend unusual
Unit 2 Grammar: Present Progressive				
• He *is wearing* a new shirt. • They *are watching* the new fashions.				

Achievement Tests
Unit 3

Name: _____

Date: _____

PART 1: LISTENING

1.1 *CD ₁ Listen to the beginning of an interview on a talk radio show. Check (✔) the best prediction of what the listening is about. There is only one right answer.*

_____ **A.** The professor of education will give his opinion about rap music.

_____ **B.** The music producer and the professor will discuss rap music.

_____ **C.** Ms. Jones and Rashawn will give their opinions about rap music.

_____ **D.** Ms. Jones will discuss rap music with the professor of education.

1.2 *CD ₁ Now listen to the entire interview. Use the information to choose the correct answers. Check (✔) the answers.*

1. The people being interviewed _____.

_____ **A.** think rappers are good examples for kids

_____ **B.** say the words in rap music are important

_____ **C.** believe rap music is good for kids

_____ **D.** have strong opinions about rap music

2. According to Ms. Jones, what percentage of male students in her neighborhood finish high school?

_____ **A.** almost fifteen percent

_____ **B.** around fifty percent

_____ **C.** forty to fifty percent

_____ **D.** about sixty percent

3. Rashawn thinks that rappers _____.

_____ **A.** stay in their neighborhoods when they become famous

_____ **B.** don't forget the place where they grew up

_____ **C.** give money to their neighborhood when they are rich

_____ **D.** don't believe it is important to finish high school

4. Ms. Jones and Rashawn most likely agree that _____.

_____ **A.** rap music has an effect on teenagers

_____ **B.** students should finish school

_____ **C.** kids should listen to rap music

_____ **D.** melody is important in rap music

5. Many rappers probably _____.

_____ **A.** play an instrument   _____ **C.** make a lot of money

_____ **B.** are good singers   _____ **D.** need to learn English

6. According to Rashawn, what is most important about rap music?

_____ **A.** the melody   _____ **C.** the songs

_____ **B.** the rhythm   _____ **D.** the singers

1.3 CD 7 *Listen to the excerpt from "Rap—Good or Bad?" from* NorthStar: Listening 12 *and Speaking* 1, *Unit 3. Use information from this listening and the listening from Part 1.2 to complete the activity. Check (✔) the box under the person who believes the statement. Not all the statements will be used. One answer is already given.*

Statements	Mr. Simon	Professor Crosby	Ms. Jones	Rashawn
A. Parents should teach their children what is right and what is wrong.	✓			
B. Teenagers can decide what is good and bad.				
C. Teenagers want to copy rappers.				
D. Rappers think that where they grew up is important.				
E. Rap music makes kids think that finishing school is not important.				
F. Rappers should show teens how important education is.				

PART 2: VOCABULARY

2.1 *Read the paragraph. Use the words from the box to fill in the blanks. Not all the words will be used.*

favorite	melody	musician	popular	rhyme
instruments	musical	play	rapper	

Rap music began in the 1970s and continues to be _____. In the

beginning of the 21st century, many people began to listen to music played

by singer-songwriters. Two things that are very important in their music are

the words and _____ of the songs so that people can sing along.

Like poetry, many of the songs include words that _____. Some

of the common _____ used by singer-songwriters include the

guitar and piano. The singers usually _____ at least one

instrument. While many new singers write this kind of music today, it comes

from one of the oldest musical forms, the folk song.

2.2 *Check (✔) the answer that best completes each sentence.*

1. A *neighborhood* is a place where people _____.

_____ **A.** work

_____ **B.** play

_____ **C.** eat

_____ **D.** live

2. To be *poor* means to _____.

_____ **A.** have a bad job

_____ **B.** be hungry

_____ **C.** have little money

_____ **D.** be without a home

3. Something that *just* happened is something that took place

   _____.

   _____ **A.** a short time ago

   _____ **B.** yesterday

   _____ **C.** before

   _____ **D.** a while ago

4. The *rhythm* of a song is the _____ or timing.

   _____ **A.** tune

   _____ **B.** beat

   _____ **C.** music

   _____ **D.** speed

5. All languages include *slang*, or language that is _____.

   _____ **A.** not formal

   _____ **B.** new

   _____ **C.** not used

   _____ **D.** simple

PART 3: SKILLS FOR SPEAKING

3.1 *Check (✔) the correct phrase to complete each sentence..*

JULIA: Hi, Antonio. What _____ to?

   _____ **A.** do you listen

   ✓ **B.** are you listening

1. ANTONIO: That new band, Freedom. _____ them?

   _____ **A.** Do you like

   _____ **B.** Are you liking

(continued on next page)

   2. JULIA: No. I hate them. When I _____ them on the
                 radio, I change the station.

   _____ **A.** hear

   _____ **B.** am hearing

   3. ANTONIO: Too bad. I _____ about seeing them in concert
                on Saturday. I guess you don't want to come then.

   _____ **A.** think

   _____ **B.** am thinking

   4. JULIA: Oh, I _____ them that much. I'd love to go.

   _____ **A.** don't hate

   _____ **B.** am not hating

3.2 CD 7 13 *Listen to the words. Check (✔) the vowel sound you hear. One answer is
            already given.*

   listen

   _____ **A.** /iy/

   ✓ **B.** /ɪ/

   1. hear

   _____ **A.** /iy/

   _____ **B.** /ɪ/

   2. bean

   _____ **A.** /iy/

   _____ **B.** /ɪ/

   3. been

   _____ **A.** /iy/

   _____ **B.** /ɪ/

3.3 *Read the conversation. Check (✔) A if the underlined phrase expresses an opinion. Check (✔) B if the phrase does not express an opinion. One answer is already given.*

SHIZUKI: What's your favorite kind of music?

KAMAR: I like just about all kinds, but I <u>usually listen to</u> rock music.

SHIZUKI: Really? (1) <u>If you ask me</u>, it's too loud and all you hear are drums and electric guitar. You can't even hear the words to the songs.

KAMAR: But that's what makes it so great. (2) <u>Don't you think</u> the new music, like the singer-songwriter stuff, is too simple? Anyone can sing a song.

SHIZUKI: Well, I like simple music. (3) <u>I think</u> it helps you relax.

usually listen to

_____ **A.**

___✓___ **B.**

1. if you ask me

_____ **A.**

_____ **B.**

2. don't you think

_____ **A.**

_____ **B.**

3. I think

_____ **A.**

_____ **B.**

PART 4: SPEAKING

4.1 *Read the statement. Check (✔) the name of the person from Part 1.2 who gave this opinion. You may listen again to Part 1.2.*

In my opinion, rappers set a good example for kids.

_____ **A.** Ms. Jones

_____ **B.** Rashawn

4.2 *Say one sentence that tells your opinion about rap music. Begin your sentence with a phrase that expresses an opinion.*

4.3 *Talking about Music*

Speak for 1–2 minutes. Give your opinion about one kind of music you like and one kind you do not like.

- Give reasons why you like or dislike each kind of music.
- Use phrases that express your opinion.
- Use the vocabulary and grammar from Unit 3.

Unit 3 Vocabulary Words			
favorite	melody	play	rhyme
great	musical instruments	poor	rhythm
just	neighborhoods	popular	slang

Unit 3 Grammar: Simple Present Tense with Non-Active (Stative) Verbs
• He ***thinks*** he ***likes*** rap music.

Achievement Tests
Unit 4

Name: _____

Date: _____

PART 1: LISTENING

1.1 CD7 (14) *Listen to the beginning of a radio commercial. Check (✔) the purpose of the commercial. There is only one right answer.*

_____ **A.** advertise that the emerald is for sale

_____ **B.** describe the history of the emerald

_____ **C.** invite people to see the emerald

_____ **D.** introduce the owner of the emerald

1.2 CD7 (15) *Now listen to the entire commercial. Use the information to choose the correct answers. Check (✔) the answers.*

1. The Mogul Emerald is one of the _____ emeralds.

_____ **A.** darkest

_____ **B.** biggest

_____ **C.** oldest

_____ **D.** most popular

2. The most important characteristic of an emerald is its

_____.

_____ **A.** cut

_____ **B.** color

_____ **C.** clarity

_____ **D.** carat

3. The Mogul Emerald is from _____.

_____ **A.** the 1300s

_____ **B.** the 1600s

_____ **C.** the 1900s

_____ **D.** 2001

(continued on next page)

4. The speaker uses all of these words to describe the Mogul Emerald

   <u>except</u> _____.

   _____ **A.** wealthy

   _____ **B.** lucky

   _____ **C.** excellent

   _____ **D.** green

5. The Mogul Emerald can be seen at the New York Museum of

   _____.

   _____ **A.** Natural History

   _____ **B.** Fine Arts

   _____ **C.** Science

   _____ **D.** Precious Stones

6. Which of the following statements does the speaker agree with?

   _____ **A.** Expensive diamonds bring bad luck.

   _____ **B.** The owner of the Mogul Emerald is not doing the right thing.

   _____ **C.** The place for a famous jewel is in the museum.

   _____ **D.** The Mogul Emerald needs to stay at the owner's home.

7. Why does the speaker tell listeners to hurry and see the Mogul Emerald?

   _____ **A.** They can meet the owner of the emerald.

   _____ **B.** They will get lucky too.

   _____ **C.** Many rich people will be there.

   _____ **D.** The emerald will not be there long.

1.3 ᶜᴰ ⑯ *Listen to an excerpt from "The Hope Diamond" from* NorthStar: Listening *and Speaking 1, Unit 4. Use information from this listening and the listening from Part 1.2 to complete the activity. Write the letter of sentence in the correct box to indicate if it is about the Mogul Emerald or the Hope Diamond. Not all the statements will be used. One answer is already given.*

~~**A.** This gemstone belonged to a king.~~

B. South Africa is the country this gemstone comes from.

C. The color of this gemstone is purple.

D. This gemstone got its name after the man who bought it.

E. People say you will have good luck if you own this gemstone.

The Hope Diamond	The Mogul Emerald
A **1.**	**2.**

PART 2: VOCABULARY

2.1 *Read an excerpt from a newspaper article about diamonds. Use the words from the box to fill in the blanks. Not all the words will be used.*

heartless	sparkle	valuable	worth
huge	steal	wealthy	

In addition to the Hope Diamond, another very famous blue diamond is the Heart of Eternity. It is only 27.64 carats—almost half of the size of the Hope Diamond. The Heart of Eternity is not as _____ as the Hope
　　　　　　　　　　　　　　　　　　　　　　　　　　　　　1.
Diamond but is very _____ because of its color. Blue diamonds
　　　　　　　　　　　2.
are very rare, and this is why many _____ people want to own
　　　　　　　　　　　　　　　　　　　　3.
them. The Heart of Eternity has an owner, but no one knows his name. Some
people say that this gemstone is _____ more than 16 million
　　　　　　　　　　　　　　　　　　4.
dollars. When the Heart of Eternity arrived in London in 2000 someone tried
to _____ it but could not.
　　　5.

2.2 *Read the rest of the article about the Heart of Eternity. Then match the words and phrases in Column A with their definitions in Column B. Write the letter of the definition on the line. Not all the definitions will be used.*

The **history** of the Heart of Eternity is not long. The Heart of Eternity is a new diamond. It was a **lucky find** for the people in the Premier Diamond Mine of South Africa. When they saw the blue color of this diamond, they knew it was **worth a fortune**. This and another blue diamond **appeared** in London in January 2000. People at the De Beers Company **advertised** the showing, and more than 12 million people came to see it.

Column A

_____ 1. history

_____ 2. lucky find

_____ 3. worth a fortune

_____ 4. appear

_____ 5. advertise

Column B

A. a chance discovery

B. good luck

C. be seen for the first time

D. let people know about something on TV, on radio, or in newspapers

E. cost a lot of money

F. bring good luck

G. things that happened in the past

H. bad luck

PART 3: SKILLS FOR SPEAKING

3.1 *Complete the conversation with the present tense of the verbs in parentheses. One answer is already given.*

SALESPERSON: How can I help you?

JOHN: I'd like to _____buy_____ a piece of jewelry for my wife.
                                (buy)

She always _____ me a perfect gift, and I need
                          1. (get)
your help to choose something special for her.

SALESPERSON: Definitely. We have a large collection in the store.

_____ your wife _____ earrings?
                                       2. (like)

JOHN: She _____ them. I was thinking of getting her a
               3. (not wear)

               ring.

SALESPERSON: I see. We have some wonderful diamond rings over here. Take

               a look.

JOHN: I like the first one on the right. It is beautiful and it

               _____. How much _____ it
               4. (sparkle)

               _____?
               5. (cost)

SALESPERSON: Actually, that one is on sale now. . . .

3.2 🎧 *Listen and circle the pronunciation of the -s ending for the underlined verbs.*

1. The guidebooks say it <u>opens</u> at nine in the morning.

    A. əz   **B.** s   **C.** z

2. I think it <u>closes</u> at five, but I'm not sure.

    A. əz   **B.** s   **C.** z

3. It <u>says</u> here that the museum's hours are nine to five.

    A. əz   **B.** s   **C.** z

4. This <u>means</u> it is better to go in the morning.

    A. əz   **B.** s   **C.** z

5. I want to check with Kelly first. Perhaps she <u>wants</u> to go shopping
    tomorrow morning.

    A. əz   **B.** s   **C.** z

PART 4: SPEAKING

4.1 *Do you think that the Mogul Emerald is lucky? Say why or why not. You may listen again to Part 1.2.*

4.2 *Do you or someone you know have something that is lucky? Say what it is and why it is lucky.*

4.3 *Lucky Gems?*

Speak for 1–2 minutes. In your opinion, can a gemstone bring good or bad luck? Explain your opinion. Give your own examples and/or examples from both listenings.

- Take notes on the listenings.
- Explain why something is good luck or bad luck.
- Use the vocabulary and grammar from Unit 4.

Unit 4 Vocabulary Words					
advertise	do the right thing	huge	selfish	tradition	weigh
appear	heartless	luck	steal	valuable	
be worth a fortune	history	lucky find	tough luck	wealthy	

Unit 4 Grammar: The Simple Present
• How much **does** the Mogul Emerald cost?   • It **costs** a lot of money.

Achievement Tests
Unit 5

Name: _____

Date: _____

PART 1: LISTENING

1.1 CD 7 ⑱ *Listen to the beginning of a poetry club meeting. Check (✔) the best prediction of what John Shaw does next. There is only one right answer.*

_____ **A.** sits down and writes a poem

_____ **B.** tells what happens at club meetings

_____ **C.** explains Alzheimer's disease

_____ **D.** explains how medical help is available

1.2 CD 7 ⑲ *Now listen to the entire meeting. Use the information to choose the correct answers. Check (✔) the answers.*

1. What is special about the poetry club?

_____ **A.** There is no other club like this.

_____ **B.** Relatives of sick people started the club.

_____ **C.** People with a disease read poems to each other.

_____ **D.** The president is a famous poet.

2. How often does the club meet?

_____ **A.** once a week

_____ **B.** twice a week

_____ **C.** once a month

_____ **D.** twice a month

3. Who is John Shaw talking to?

_____ **A.** people with Alzheimer's disease

_____ **B.** relatives of people with Alzheimer's

_____ **C.** people with Alzheimer's and their families

_____ **D.** people with Alzheimer's and their doctors

(continued on next page)

4. When the woman first asks about her mother, she thinks

   _____.

   _____ **A.** her mother does not remember how to read

   _____ **B.** her mother cannot write poetry

   _____ **C.** John Shaw can help her mother

   _____ **D.** only doctors and nurses can help her mother

5. John Shaw mentioned that people with Alzheimer's like the club because

   they _____.

   _____ **A.** make friends

   _____ **B.** recover lost memories

   _____ **C.** feel amazing

   _____ **D.** return every week

6. One group member talked about what happened in _____.

   _____ **A.** Rio

   _____ **B.** Athens

   _____ **C.** Paris

   _____ **D.** Rome

1.3 🔊 *Listen to an excerpt from "I Remember" from* NorthStar: Listening and
(20) Speaking 1, *Unit 5. Use information from this listening and the listening from
Part 1.2 to complete the activity. Circle three more sentences that describe
the members of both groups.*

A. have Alzheimer's disease

B. need constant medical help

C. revise and edit stories / poems

D. write stories / poems

E. read stories / poems

F. feel happy

PART 2: VOCABULARY

2.1   *Read the sentences. Use the words and phrases from the box to fill in the blanks. Not all the words and phrases will be used.*

by yourself	hang out with	on my own
enjoy myself	make new friends	with friends

1. Did you go out _____ when your friends weren't home?

2. I don't like to study in groups with other students. I prefer to study _____ when I'm alone in my room.

3. Lee enjoys playing computer games _____. Playing alone is not fun for him.

4. My sister likes to _____ at parties.

2.2   *Read the sentences. Then match the words and phrases in Column A with their definitions in Column B. Write the letter of the definition on the line. Not all the definitions will be used.*

Grandma does not **remember** where she left her keys. She often loses things.

Tom's father has a bad **memory**. He **gets lost** in his own neighborhood.

Many elderly people are very **lonely** and have no friends to **get together** with. That is why some of them **join** different clubs.

Column A

_____ 1. remember

_____ 2. memory

_____ 3. get lost

_____ 4. lonely

_____ 5. get together

_____ 6. join

Column B

A. afraid to be alone

B. be unable to find the way

C. become a member

D. gather

E. sad to be alone

F. keep in mind

G. illness

H. ability to recall events

PART 3: SKILLS FOR SPEAKING

3.1 *Complete the conversations using the words in parentheses. Use **want, like** and **need** with a second verb in the infinitive form (**want / like / need + to write**). One answer is already given.*

   A: Have you heard that Tom Cruise's new movie starts tomorrow?

   B: We _____*need to go*_____ (need, go) see it!

1. **A:** What _____ (you like, do) on vacation?

   B: I like to lie on the beach. How about you?

2. **A:** Why are you washing dishes by yourself?

   B: Sean is angry with me. He _____ (not want, help) me.

3. **A:** Do you know why Phil and Miranda study so hard?

   B: They _____ (want, get) good grades.

4. **A:** Why _____ (Jim need, buy) a second car?

   B: Because his wife drives the other one.

3.2 🔘 CD *Listen to each sentence and the repeated word. Decide whether the word contains the /ey/ sound (as in br**ea**k) or the /ɛ/ sound (as in br**ea**kfast). Check (✔) the appropriate column. One answer is already given.*

Word	/ey/	/ɛ/
help		✓
1. make		
2. bed		
3. again		
4. place		
5. day		
6. better		

PART 4: SPEAKING

4.1 *Say one way the poetry club from Part 1.2 helps elderly people not to feel lonely and sad. You may listen again to Part 1.2.*

4.2 *What things do you like to do? Say one thing that you like to do and explain why, using phrases you learned in the unit.*

4.3 *Speak for 1–2 minutes. What else can elderly people do not to feel lonely and sad? Describe two activities they could do.*

- Take notes.
- Use expressions for saying what you like and don't like.
- Ask students to interrupt politely to ask questions.
- Use the vocabulary and grammar from Unit 5.

Unit 5 Vocabulary Words		
disease	get together	lose
feel lonely	group member	memories
forget	hang out	relative
get lost	join	

Unit 5 Grammar: *Like to / Want to / Need to*
• What do the elderly *like / want / need to do*?   • They *like / want / need to get together* with friends.

Achievement Tests
Unit 6

Name: _____

Date: _____

PART 1: LISTENING

1.1 _CD_
(22) *Listen to the beginning of a class discussion. Check (✔) the best prediction of what the listening is about. There is only one right answer.*

_____ **A.** why it is not easy to be creative in business

_____ **B.** where to start a new business

_____ **C.** when is a good time to start a business

_____ **D.** who will be successful in business

1.2 _CD_
(23) *Now listen to the entire discussion. Use the information to choose the correct answers. Check (✔) the answers.*

1. Dr. Kim says it is hard to _____.

_____ **A.** buy things you need

_____ **B.** start a new business

_____ **C.** think of new things to sell

_____ **D.** work too many hours

2. The new kind of bicycle _____.

_____ **A.** is very safe   _____ **C.** has a new seat

_____ **B.** is very large   _____ **D.** has four wheels

3. What did Martin make?

_____ **A.** a toy   _____ **C.** a pencil

_____ **B.** a bicycle   _____ **D.** a wheel

4. How old was Martin when he started his business?

_____ **A.** seven   _____ **C.** ten

_____ **B.** eight   _____ **D.** twelve

5. Dr. Kim most likely thinks kids _____.

_____ **A.** have more free time than adults

_____ **B.** are more afraid than adults

_____ **C.** are less creative than adults

_____ **D.** make fewer mistakes than adults

CD 1 24 *Listen again to a part of the discussion. Then answer the question.*

6. What does the student mean when he says: "Right, relax"?

_____ **A.** He agrees with the professor.

_____ **B.** He is answering the professor

_____ **C.** He doesn't think he can relax.

_____ **D.** He doesn't think it's good to relax.

1.3 **CD 1 25** *Listen to an excerpt from "A Business Class" from* NorthStar: Listening and Speaking 1, *Unit 6. Use the information from this listening and the listening from Part 1.2 to complete the activity. For each person, write the letter of the word or phrase that completes each sentence.*

A. act like a child

B. never bring work home

C. meditate

D. don't have free time

E. don't have a good time

~~**F.** are afraid~~

	Professor Ray	Dr. Kim
It's hard to be creative if you _____.	F	2.
To be more creative _____.	1.	3.

PART 2: VOCABULARY

2.1 *Read the paragraph. Use the words and phrases from the box to fill in the blanks. Not all the words and phrases will be used.*

business	co-workers	feature	owner
come up with	exciting	improve creativity	work experience

We are looking for ten people who can work hard and want to be part of

a(n) _____ new company. These people must be able to
   1.

_____ ideas to _____ at our company. They must
   2.   **3.**

have at least five years of _____. If you are interested, please call
                              4.

Mr. Simon, the _____ of the company, at (619) 555-9989.
                  5.

2.2 *Check (✔) the answer that best completes each sentence.*

1. A business that is *successful* _____.

   _____ **A.** makes money   _____ **C.** needs employees

   _____ **B.** isn't creative   _____ **D.** has problems

2. To *try* means to _____.

   _____ **A.** want to   _____ **C.** attempt to

   _____ **B.** be able to   _____ **D.** have to

3. A *feature* on a new product is something that makes it

   _____.

   _____ **A.** different or special   _____ **C.** new and pretty

   _____ **B.** more expensive   _____ **D.** very creative

4. To *get around* means to _____.

   _____ **A.** meet people face-to-face

   _____ **B.** go from one place to another place

   _____ **C.** talk to each of your friends or co-workers

   _____ **D.** find out answers to questions

5. To *make a mistake* means to _____.

_____ **A.** have a bad time

_____ **B.** say something impolite

_____ **C.** make a person mad

_____ **D.** do something wrong

PART 3: SKILLS FOR SPEAKING

3.1 *Read the conversation. Use the phrases from the box to fill in the blanks. Not all the phrases will be used. The first one has been done for you.*

are there	there are	there were	was there
is there	there was	was there	

BILL: ____Is there____ a meeting in a couple hours?

ROSEMARY: Oh, yes, but I don't know anything about it. Where will the

meeting be?

BILL: I'm not sure. _____ some information about it in
                                    1.

the e-mail we got yesterday.

ROSEMARY: Oh, I remember. This is the meeting about improving creativity

in our company. Last year _____ only two successful
                                         2.

new products.

BILL: _____ a few new ideas that the company is planning
                  3.

to start this year?

ROSEMARY: I think so. Uh-oh, _____ only two hours until the
                                       4.

meeting starts. I still need to do some work.

3.2 🔘 *Listen to the sentences. The first word in each sentence contains either a voiceless "th" sound (as in **thanks**) or a voiced "th" sound (as in **this**). Check (✔) the correct answer. The first one has been done for you.*

<u>The</u> owner of the company will visit tomorrow.

_____ **A.** voiceless   _✓_ **B.** voiced

1. <u>Think</u> about how to improve creativity.

_____ **A.** voiceless   _____ **B.** voiced

2. <u>There</u> are two new employees.

_____ **A.** voiceless   _____ **B.** voiced

3. <u>Thursday</u> we had a meeting.

_____ **A.** voiceless   _____ **B.** voiced

3.3 *Read the conversations. Check (✔) the best response. The first one has been done for you.*

A: So what do you do?

B: I'm an actor, but now I'm working in a restaurant.

A: _____

_✓_ **A.** Uh-huh.   _____ **B.** Wow!   _____ **C.** That's great!

1. **A:** This is my office.

B: Your office is in the Empire State Building?

A: Yes, I can look out the window and see the whole city!

B: _____

_____ **A.** Uh-huh.   _____ **B.** Wow!   _____ **C.** That's interesting.

2. **A:** How do you like working at the United Nations?

B: I like it. One of my co-workers is from Nigeria, one is from Thailand, and one is from Russia.

A: _____

_____ **A.** Uh-huh.   _____ **B.** Wow!   _____ **C.** That's interesting.

3. A: I love my new job! We can start work any time between 8:00 a.m. and noon, and we don't work on Mondays or Fridays. And we even get three months of vacation a year!

    B: _____

_____ **A.** Uh-huh.   _____ **B.** That's great!   _____ **C.** That's interesting.

PART 4: SPEAKING

4.1 *Tell what new product Martin Green from Part 1.2 made. You may listen again to Part 1.2.*

4.2 *Say what you think about the product Martin Green made. Use an expression that shows your interest in this product.*

4.3 *Talking about a New Product*

Speak for 1–2 minutes. Imagine you work for a company that needs a new product. You have come up with a creative product. Tell the owner of the company about this product.

- Take notes.
- Name your product and describe what it looks like and what it does.
- Tell the owner how it will help the company.
- Use *there is* and *there are* in your description.
- Use the vocabulary and grammar from Unit 6.

Unit 6 Vocabulary Words			
afraid	exciting	improve creativity	owner
business	feature	make a mistake	try
come up with	get around	successful	work experience

Unit 6 Grammar: *There is / There are / There was / There were*
• *There is* a new feature on this product. • *There are* several reasons why it is difficult for adults to be creative.

PART 1: LISTENING

1.1 🎧 *CD 7 27* *Listen to the beginning of a conversation. Check (✔) the best prediction of what the listening is about. There is only one right answer.*

_____ **A.** when Ruth Davidow came to the United States

_____ **B.** why Ruth Davidow is important

_____ **C.** why Ruth Davidow won a Nobel Peace Prize

_____ **D.** what Ruth Davidow studied

1.2 🎧 *CD 7 28* *Now listen to the entire conversation. Use the information to choose the correct answers. Check (✔) the answers.*

1. Ruth Davidow was a _____.

_____ **A.** nurse

_____ **B.** soldier

_____ **C.** politician

_____ **D.** teacher

2. She helped fight for _____.

_____ **A.** Abraham Lincoln

_____ **B.** democracy in Spain

_____ **C.** democracy in the United States

_____ **D.** Franco

3. About how many Americans were killed in the fight against Franco?

_____ **A.** 300

_____ **B.** 900

_____ **C.** 1,900

_____ **D.** 3,000

4. What did Ruth Davidow do in 1965?

_____ **A.** She fought for democracy in China.

_____ **B.** She fought for equal rights for women.

_____ **C.** She protested for civil rights in the United States.

_____ **D.** She helped fight for democracy in Africa.

5. How old was Ruth Davidow when she was in China?

_____ **A.** 80

_____ **B.** 85

_____ **C.** 88

_____ **D.** 90

6. Naomi's friend Jackie probably thinks that Ruth Davidow is

_____.

_____ **A.** shocking

_____ **B.** funny

_____ **C.** amusing

_____ **D.** courageous

1.3 CD 7 / 29 *Listen to "Rigoberta Menchu, a Mayan Leader" from* NorthStar: Listening *and Speaking 1, Unit 7. Use the information from this listening and the listening from Part 1.2 to complete the activity. One answer is already given.*

~~**A.** fought for the democracy of her country~~

B. fought for the democracy of a different country

C. fought for the Civil Rights Movement in Mexico

D. "We must fight for change if there is injustice."

E. "We have learned that change cannot come through war."

F. "I can't live in the world if I can't fight against injustice."

	Rigoberta Menchu	**Ruth Davidow**
What she did	A	**2.**
What she said	**1.**	**3.**

PART 2: VOCABULARY

2.1 *Read the paragraph. Use the words and phrases from the box to fill in the blanks. Not all the words and phrases will be used.*

democracy	jail	protest against	stood up for	violence
had courage	plant	shocked	take care of it	

The United States is a _____, but African Americans did not

_____1._____

always have equal rights. People began to _____ this problem in

_____2._____

1955. They _____ and fought against the government. A leader

_____3._____

in this fight was Martin Luther King, Jr. He _____ the equal

_____4._____

rights of all people. He did not believe in _____. In 1968 people

_____5._____

were _____ when Martin Luther King was shot. This was not

_____6._____

the end of the fight.

2.2 *Check (✔) the answer that best completes each sentence.*

1. To *speak out about* a problem means to _____ it.

   _____ **A.** take action against

   _____ **B.** want to do

   _____ **C.** tell someone about

   _____ **D.** try to do

2. A *political* fight is about a problem with the _____.

   _____ **A.** family

   _____ **B.** church

   _____ **C.** police

   _____ **D.** government

    3. To *fight for* means to _____.

        _____ **A.** talk quietly about

        _____ **B.** act strongly against

        _____ **C.** hope for

        _____ **D.** dream of

    4. To *care about* something means to _____.

        _____ **A.** want it to do well

        _____ **B.** see it differently

        _____ **C.** hope it is strong

        _____ **D.** feel it is there

PART 3: SKILLS FOR SPEAKING

3.1 *Read the conversation. Fill in the blanks with the correct form of the verb. One answer is already given.*

JACKIE: I wasn't in class yesterday. _____Did you hear_____ Johanna's talk?
                                                    (you hear)

NAOMI: Yes. She _____ about Martin Luther King.
                         1. (speak)

JACKIE: _____ for equal rights for African Americans?
            2. (he fight)

NAOMI: Yes. I _____ a lot about him. He _____ in
                    3. (learn)   **4.** (not believe)
        violence.

3.2 CD7 *Listen to the words. Check (✔) the past tense ending you hear. One answer is already given.*

    lived

    __✓__ **A.** /d/   _____ **B.** /t/   _____ **C.** /ɪd/

  1. wanted

    _____ **A.** /d/   _____ **B.** /t/   _____ **C.** /ɪd/

(continued on next page)

2. planted

_____ **A.** /d/   _____ **B.** /t/   _____ **C.** /ɪd/

3. watched

_____ **A.** /d/   _____ **B.** /t/   _____ **C.** /ɪd/

3.3 *Read the sentences. Check (✔) the answer that best completes each sentence. One answer is already given.*

Ruth Davidow fought for democracy. Rigoberta fought for democracy.

Ruth Davidow fought for democracy, and Rigoberta Menchu _____.

_✓_ **A.** did, too   _____ **C.** was, too

_____ **B.** didn't either   _____ **D.** wasn't either

1. Ruth Davidow and Martin Luther King were not afraid to fight for equal rights. Wangari Maathai and Rigoberta Menchu were not afraid to fight for equal rights.

   Davidow and King were not afraid to fight for equal rights, and Maathai and Menchu _____.

   _____ **A.** was, too   _____ **C.** wasn't either

   _____ **B.** were, too   _____ **D.** weren't either

2. Martin Luther King believed in nonviolence. Rigoberta Menchu believed in nonviolence.

   King believed in nonviolence, and Menchu _____.

   _____ **A.** did, too   _____ **C.** was, too

   _____ **B.** didn't either   _____ **D.** wasn't either

3. Rigoberta was a strong woman. Wangari was a strong woman.

   Rigoberta was a strong woman, and Wangari _____.

   _____ **A.** did, too   _____ **C.** was, too

   _____ **B.** didn't either   _____ **D.** wasn't either

PART 4: SPEAKING

4.1 *Say something Ruth Davidow did that is similar to something Rigoberta Menchu did.*

4.2 *Use a phrase that expresses similarity between Ruth Davidow and Rigoberta Menchu.*

4.3 *Two Powerful Women*

Speak for 1–2 minutes. Compare the lives of Ruth Davidow and Rigoberta Menchu.

- Take notes.
- Talk about how these two people were similar.
- Use the simple past tense.
- Use phrases for expressing similarities and differences.
- Use the vocabulary and grammar from Unit 7.

Unit 7 Vocabulary Words				
cared for	dreamed of	political	shocked	violence
democracy	had courage	political power	spoke out about	were against
destroy	jail	protest against	stood up for	

Unit 7 Grammar: Simple Past Tense
• She **wanted** to help. • He **became** a leader. • She **stopped** studying.

Achievement Tests
Unit 8

Name: _____

Date: _____

PART 1: LISTENING

1.1 $\overset{CD}{31}$ *Listen to the beginning of a conversation. Check (✔) the best prediction of what the listening is about. There is only one right answer.*

_____ **A.** how dangerous road rage is

_____ **B.** how common road rage is

_____ **C.** how a psychologist can treat road rage

_____ **D.** how traffic school can help road rage

1.2 $\overset{CD}{32}$ *Now listen to the entire conversation. Use the information to choose the correct answers. Check (✔) the answers.*

1. The psychologist wants to _____.

   _____ **A.** take away Mr. Hansen's driver's license

   _____ **B.** teach Mr. Hansen good manners

   _____ **C.** find out why Mr. Hansen can't control his anger

   _____ **D.** show Mr. Hansen how to drive more politely

2. How many times did Mr. Hansen go to traffic school?

   _____ **A.** 1

   _____ **B.** 2

   _____ **C.** 3

   _____ **D.** 4

3. Mr. Hansen got angry the first time because _____.

   _____ **A.** a car didn't go at a green light

   _____ **B.** a driver honked at him

   _____ **C.** a car was tailgating him

   _____ **D.** a driver was arguing with his wife

4. Why was Mr. Hansen in traffic school the second time?

_____ **A.** He was tailgating.

_____ **B.** He was changing lanes.

_____ **C.** A driver wasn't paying attention to him.

_____ **D.** A driver argued with him.

🔘 **CD 1 33** *Listen again to an excerpt from the conversation. Then answer the question.*

5. Why does the psychologist say "Hmm, I think this is going to be difficult"?

_____ **A.** She thinks she can't help Mr. Hansen.

_____ **B.** She thinks it will not be easy to help Mr. Hansen.

_____ **C.** Mr. Hansen will get angry.

_____ **D.** Mr. Hansen doesn't think traffic school is easy.

6. Mr. Hansen will most likely _____.

_____ **A.** go back to traffic school

_____ **B.** be a safer driver

_____ **C.** lose his driver's license

_____ **D.** lose his car

1.3 🔘 **CD 1 34** *Listen to "Driving Phobia" from* NorthStar: Listening and Speaking 1, *Unit 8. Use the information from this listening and the listening from Part 1.2 to complete the activity. One answer is already given.*

A. angry

B. energetic

C. ~~encouraging~~

D. excited

E. insecure

F. frustrated

	Conversation with Allen	**Conversation with Mr. Hansen**
Psychologist's attitude	C	2.
Patient's feelings	1.	3.

PART 2: VOCABULARY

2.1 *Read the interview. Use the words from the box to fill in the blanks. Not all the words will be used.*

anonymous	intersection	rude
control	lane	signal
crowded	paying attention	tailgating
honks	polite	
injured	psychologist	

INTERVIEWER: Road rage is a major problem today. Some people cannot

_____ their anger when they drive. They can be
          1.

very _____ to other drivers. Dr. Jones is a
          2.

_____ who helps people deal with their anger.
          3.

Dr. Jones, please give us an example of road rage.

DR. JONES: A driver might be at an _____. Perhaps he isn't
                                        4.

_____, so he doesn't see the light turn to green.
          5.

The driver behind him gets so angry she _____
                                                        6.

her horn or even yells at the other driver.

INTERVIEWER: Some people are not very _____, but is this
                                            7.

dangerous?

DR. JONES: Road rage can be very dangerous. For example, freeways today

are often _____. A person who is in a hurry
          8.

might change to a faster _____. If there is a car in
                              9.

front of him, he might drive right behind that car. This is

called _____. It can cause accidents on the
          10.

freeway.

PART 3: SKILLS FOR SPEAKING

3.1 *Complete the conversation. Fill in the blanks using the simple past or past progressive. One answer is already given.*

OFFICER: How did this accident happen?

DRIVER: When the light turned red, I ____*stopped*____ at the intersection.
(stop)

The car behind me _____ the red light. I don't think
1. (not see)

he _____ while he was driving. In fact, he
2. (pay attention)

_____ on the phone. Before he could stop, he
3. (talk)

_____ my car. Luckily, no one was injured.
4. (hit)

3.2 CD 7 *Listen to the sentences. Check (✔) the number of thought groups you hear.*
35 *One answer is already given.*

Be careful when driving in the rain.

_____ **A.** 1   ✓ **B.** 2   _____ **C.** 3

1. Stop when the light turns green.

_____ **A.** 1   _____ **B.** 2   _____ **C.** 3

2. The car was going too fast to stop.

_____ **A.** 1   _____ **B.** 2   _____ **C.** 3

3. Never talk on the phone while driving.

_____ **A.** 1   _____ **B.** 2   _____ **C.** 3

4. A police officer can take your driver's license away.

_____ **A.** 1   _____ **B.** 2   _____ **C.** 3

5. Don't you think tailgating is dangerous?

_____ **A.** 1   _____ **B.** 2   _____ **C.** 3

6. I don't see it that way.

_____ **A.** 1   _____ **B.** 2   _____ **C.** 3

PART 4: SPEAKING

4.1 *Say one reason that Mr. Hansen from Part 1.2 gives for honking at another car. You may listen again to Part 1.2.*

4.2 *Say something to disagree with Mr. Hansen. Use an expression to show you have a different opinion.*

4.3 *Talking about a Problem*

Pretend you have to talk to Mr. Hansen about his dangerous driving.

- Tell what Mr. Hansen says about his driving.
- Tell Mr. Hansen that you have a different opinion.
- Use an expression to show that you have a different point of view from Mr. Hansen.
- Use the vocabulary and grammar from Unit 8.

Unit 8 Vocabulary Words			
anonymous	honks	officer	refuse
control	injured	paying attention	rude
crowded	intersection	polite	signal
frustrated	lane	psychologist	tailgating

Unit 8 Grammar: Simple Past and Past Progressive
[simple past] • Mr. Hansen **honked** at the driver. [past progressive]   [simple past] • The driver **was thinking** about something when the light **turned** green.

Achievement Tests
Unit 9

Name: _____

Date: _____

PART 1: LISTENING

1.1 CD7 (36) *Listen to the beginning of a radio show. Check (✔) the best prediction of what the listening is about. There is only one right answer.*

_____ **A.** only children and their parents

_____ **B.** families without children

_____ **C.** children with brothers and sisters

_____ **D.** parents and their children

1.2 CD7 (37) *Now listen to the entire show. Use the information to choose the correct answers. Check (✔) the answers.*

1. Maria Sanchez is talking to _____.

_____ **A.** a brother and his sister

_____ **B.** two only children

_____ **C.** a family with two boys and two girls

_____ **D.** a girl and a boy from different families

2. How many children are in Alicia's family?

_____ **A.** 1

_____ **B.** 2

_____ **C.** 3

_____ **D.** 4

3. Alicia's father says he _____.

_____ **A.** wants another child

_____ **B.** can't afford another child

_____ **C.** is too old for more children

_____ **D.** has too many children

(continued on next page)

4. Maria Sanchez most likely thinks that some day Alicia will

   _____.

   _____ **A.** be glad she has brothers

   _____ **B.** want to be an only child

   _____ **C.** not want a sister

   _____ **D.** not like her brothers

5. Vincent says he _____.

   _____ **A.** sometimes feels lonely

   _____ **B.** wants another brother

   _____ **C.** is the oldest child

   _____ **D.** gets tired of his siblings

6. Maria Sanchez thinks that _____.

   _____ **A.** a family with five children is unusual

   _____ **B.** five children are too many

   _____ **C.** it is too expensive to have five children

   _____ **D.** children from big families are special

1.3 🔊 *Listen to the excerpt from "How Do Only Kids Feel?" from* NorthStar:
   *Listening and Speaking 1, Unit 9. Use the information from this listening
   and the listening from Part 1.2 to complete the activity. Put the letters of the
   statements in the correct boxes. Not all the statements will be used. One
   answer is already given.*

   A. I don't get along with my brother.

   ~~**B.** My parents spend a lot of time with me.~~

   C. We can't afford to travel.

   D. I'm never alone.

   E. I want a sister.

   F. I'm not like the other kids at school.

Jay	Tonia	Jay and Vincent	Tonia and Alicia
B			

PART 2: VOCABULARY

2.1 *Read the paragraph. Use the words and phrases from the box to fill in the blanks. Not all the words and phrases will be used.*

afford	get along with	make money	spoiled
busy	hard	siblings	take care of

Many people today cannot _____ to have a lot of children. They

can only _____ one child, so there are many children without
         2.

_____. Some people think that only children are
  3.

_____. They think only children do not _____
  4.   **5.**

other children.

2.2 *Check (✔) the answer that best completes each sentence.*

1. *Selfish* people think only about _____.

_____ **A.** themselves   _____ **C.** their siblings

_____ **B.** other people   _____ **D.** their parents

2. It is *especially* hot means it is _____ hot.

_____ **A.** a little   _____ **C.** not

_____ **B.** too   _____ **D.** very

3. If you are *tired* it is hard to _____.

_____ **A.** work   _____ **C.** eat

_____ **B.** sleep   _____ **D.** laugh

4. To *raise* a child means to _____ him.

_____ **A.** grow   _____ **C.** be interested in

_____ **B.** take care of   _____ **D.** listen to

5. *Self-confident* people believe they _____.

_____ **A.** can do things well _____ **C.** do not have problems

_____ **B.** are helpful   _____ **D.** need help

PART 3: SKILLS FOR SPEAKING

3.1 *Complete the sentences. Fill in the blanks with the correct form of **be going to** and the words in parentheses. One answer is already given.*

A: When _____ are you going to get married _____?

(you, get married)

B: In June. _____ a big wedding. Sam has a lot

1. (it, be)

of brothers and sisters, and they all have children.

A: How about you and Sam? _____ children?

2. (have)

B: No, _____. We both travel a lot, and Sam

3. (not, short form)

_____ law school next year.

4. (start)

3.2 CD 7 39 *Listen to the sentences. Check (✔) the form of **going to** that you hear. One answer is already given.*

Today we're <u>going to</u> discuss families with only one child.

____✓____ **A.** /gówŋ tə/   _____ **B.** /gə́nə/

1. We're <u>going to</u> wait a year until we have children.

   _____ **A.** /gówŋ tə/   _____ **B.** /gə́nə/

2. I work during the day, so my mom is <u>going to</u> take care of the kids.

   _____ **A.** /gówŋ tə/   _____ **B.** /gə́nə/

3. It's not <u>going to</u> be easy to raise your child by yourself.

   _____ **A.** /gówŋ tə/   _____ **B.** /gə́nə/

3.3 *Read the conversation. Check (✔) the answer that best completes each sentence. One answer is already given.*

MARIA: Some people say children need siblings. What do you think?

TERESA: _____. I hate being an only child!

  ✔   **A.** That's for sure.

_____ **B.** I disagree.

_____ **C.** I'm not sure about that.

SERENA: _____. I'm an only child, and I never feel lonely.
      1.

_____ **A.** I agree.

_____ **B.** I don't agree.

_____ **C.** Hmm . . . maybe.

MARIA: A study shows that only children are spoiled.

TERESA: _____. I don't think I'm spoiled.
      2.

_____ **A.** I agree.

_____ **B.** I think that's true.

_____ **C.** I don't agree.

MARIA: _____. You're not spoiled.
      3.

_____ **A.** That's true.

_____ **B.** I don't think that's true.

_____ **C.** Hmm . . . maybe.

PART 4: SPEAKING

4.1 *Check (✔) one thing the studies from Part 1.2 showed. You may listen again to Part 1.2.*

_____ **A.** Children with siblings are less intelligent.

_____ **B.** Children with siblings are less selfish.

_____ **C.** Children with siblings are less happy.

4.2 *Say whether you agree or disagree with the answer in 4.1. Use an expression from the unit to tell your opinion.*

4.3 *Discussing Pros and Cons*

Speak for 1–2 minutes. Talk about the pros (positive points) and cons (negative points) of being an only child and being a child with siblings.

- Take notes.
- Use some of the information from the listenings.
- Use the verb *going to* to begin your talk.
- Use expressions of agreement and disagreement.
- Use the vocabulary and grammar from Unit 9.

Unit 9 Vocabulary Words			
afford	get along with	self-confident	spoiled
busy	independent	selfish	take care of
especially	raise	siblings	tired

Unit 9 Grammar: The Future with *Be Going To*
• James and Kelly **are going to** get married in May. • **Are** they **going to** have any children? • They **aren't going to** have children.

Achievement Tests
Unit 10

Name: _____

Date: _____

PART 1: LISTENING

1.1 CD7 *Listen to the beginning of a radio call-in show. Check (✔) the best prediction*
40 *of what the listening is about. There is only one right answer.*

_____ **A.** how many people play soccer in the world

_____ **B.** what countries have a national sport

_____ **C.** why people around the world watch sports

_____ **D.** what the national sports around the world are

1.2 CD7 *Now listen to the entire radio show. Use the information to choose the*
41 *correct answers. Check (✔) the answers.*

1. People around the world like _____.

_____ **A.** basketball

_____ **B.** soccer

_____ **C.** baseball

_____ **D.** rugby

2. The man from England _____.

_____ **A.** likes baseball

_____ **B.** likes rugby

_____ **C.** plays soccer

_____ **D.** plays rugby

3. The host most likely thinks _____.

_____ **A.** rugby should not be the national sport of England

_____ **B.** James should go to more rugby matches

_____ **C.** national sports are important

_____ **D.** watching sports is very expensive

(continued on next page)

4. The French man says that _____.

_____ A. all French children can play soccer

_____ B. all French people understand baseball

_____ C. soccer is the perfect sport

_____ D. soccer is the universal sport

5. The woman from Spain most likely _____.

_____ A. thinks the French have the perfect soccer team

_____ B. thinks bullfighting is too cruel

_____ C. does not like bullfighting very much

_____ D. does not usually agree with the French

6. The woman from Spain thinks _____.

_____ A. soccer is a good sport for children

_____ B. people should understand the beauty of soccer

_____ C. baseball is an exciting sport

_____ D. soccer is the national sport of Spain

1.3 ⊙ *Listen to the excerpt from "America Talks" from* NorthStar: Listening and
Speaking 1, *Unit 10. Use the information from this listening and the listening
from Part 1.2 to complete the activity.*

A. rugby

B. soccer

~~C. baseball~~

D. It is a tradition in this country.

E. It's too expensive.

F. The scores aren't very high.

	Steve	**Jean-Pierre**
What sport was he talking about?	C	2.
What did he say about it?	1.	3.

PART 2: VOCABULARY

2.1 *Read the paragraph. Use the words from the box to fill in the blanks. Not all the words will be used.*

fans	nationalities	score	ties
match	rules	team	universal

People around the world like soccer, so it is a _____ sport.

1.

Soccer _____ watch their country play this sport. Each country

2.

has its own _____. The biggest soccer _____ is the

3.   4.

World Cup. People of many _____ watch the World Cup.

5.

2.2 *Check (✔) the answer that best completes each sentence.*

1. People play soccer on a soccer _____.

   _____ **A.** land   _____ **C.** field

   _____ **B.** place   _____ **D.** country

2. Some people think soccer is the _____ sport.

   _____ **A.** perfect   _____ **C.** easy

   _____ **B.** good   _____ **D.** nice

3. A soccer ball and a goal are all the _____ you need to play soccer.

   _____ **A.** equipment   _____ **C.** furniture

   _____ **B.** teams   _____ **D.** toys

4. When a soccer team gets a point, people yell "_____."

   _____ **A.** win   _____ **C.** great

   _____ **B.** goal   _____ **D.** play

5. The _____ in a soccer game might not be very high.

   _____ **A.** people   _____ **C.** players

   _____ **B.** number   _____ **D.** score

PART 3: SKILLS FOR SPEAKING

3.1 *Use the words to make sentences using* should. *One answer is already given.*

Every boy or girl/ learn/ how to play soccer.

Every boy or girl should learn how to play soccer. _____

1. It / not be / very important / to score a lot of points.

    _____

2. Americans / watch / more soccer.

    _____

3. You / wear / the right clothes / to play soccer.

    _____

4. A sport / be fun / to play.

    _____

3.2 _{CD 1 43} *Listen to the sentences. Check (✔) the phrase that stresses the meaning of the sentences. One answer is already given.*

I need new soccer shoes.

   __✓__ **A.** not my brother

   _____ **B.** not old soccer shoes

   _____ **C.** not equipment

1. There are nine players on a baseball team.

   _____ **A.** not ten

   _____ **B.** not on a basketball team

   _____ **C.** not on a baseball field

2. I said you should be home by six o'clock.

   _____ **A.** not your sister

   _____ **B.** not at the soccer field

   _____ **C.** not seven o'clock

3. Our team is playing baseball on this field.

_____ **A.** not your team

_____ **B.** not soccer

_____ **C.** not that field

3.3 *Check (✔) the answer that best completes each sentence. One answer is already given.*

I watched the World Cup _____ it is exciting.

_____ **A.** so   ✓ **B.** because

1. The weather was perfect for skiing. _____ I went skiing.

_____ **A.** That's why   _____ **B.** Because

2. The best player was sick, _____ he didn't play.

_____ **A.** because   _____ **B.** so

3. The game tonight is going to be good. _____ Tom is going to watch it.

_____ **A.** Because   _____ **B.** That's why

PART 4: SPEAKING

4.1 *Say why the French man and the Spanish woman from Part 1.2 do not like baseball. You may listen again to Part 1.2.*

4.2 *State one of the following:*

- *a reason why you don't like baseball other than the reason given in 4.1. Use an expression to introduce your reason.*

OR

- *the fact that you like baseball. Use an expression to introduce a result of this fact.*

4.3 *Talking about Your Favorite Sport*

Speak for 1–2 minutes. Tell why you like a sport.
- Take notes.
- Tell about several rules of this sport using *should* or *should not*.
- Emphasize the important words in the sentences.
- Use the vocabulary and grammar from Unit 10.

Unit 10 Vocabulary Words			
fans	match	rules	ties
field	nationalities	score	universal
goal	perfect score	team	
Unit 10 Grammar: *Should* for Ideas and Opinions			
• You ***should*** learn the rules of baseball. • Baseball ***shouldn't*** be difficult to learn.			

Achievement Tests Audioscript

UNIT 1

1.1

Study Abroad Director: Good morning, everyone. This is Don. He spent last year in Frankfurt, Germany. He's here to tell you about his study abroad experience.

Don: Hello. I am twenty years old, and I'm a senior here at Boston University. I'm from New York. I'm glad you're interested in studying abroad. I had an amazing time in Germany. Who wants to ask the first question?

1.2

Study Abroad Director: Good morning, everyone. This is Don. He spent last year in Frankfurt, Germany. He's here to tell you about his study abroad experience.

Don: Hello. I am twenty years old, and I'm a senior here at Boston University. I'm from New York. I'm glad you're interested in studying abroad. I had an amazing time in Germany. Who wants to ask the first question?

Student 1: I have a question. Why did you go to Germany?

Don: I study history and German. I wanted to improve my German and learn more about the culture of Germany.

Student 2: Where did you live?

Don: I stayed with a wonderful host family. They lived very close to the university. From the beginning, I felt like I was their son.

Student 1: Did you have problems speaking with them?

Don: At first, it was hard. My host family spoke a little English, but many of the students at the university spoke only German. Everyone spoke very fast. It was hard to understand, but it got easier. I made many German friends. Now we e-mail each other in German every week. My German is great.

Student 3: Did you have time to travel?

Don: Yes, I did! I traveled all around Germany. I also visited Belgium, France, and the Czech Republic.

Student 2: I'm so excited about studying abroad. I'm very interested in international cultures. What do I do first?

Don: First, fill out an application. You can go to the study abroad website and fill out the application online. Good luck to all of you!

1.3

Annie: Oh, I loved my host family in Costa Rica. They were so wonderful. They were my family too! From the first day, I felt like I was their daughter. They called me "Ana."

Interviewer: That's so nice. Did you have any problems speaking with them?

Annie: No, not really. At first, I didn't speak much Spanish, and they spoke only a little English. But I learned a lot of

Spanish from them, and in my Spanish class too. And I also learned that language is not always so important!

Interviewer: What do you mean?

Annie: Well, you know, sometimes a smile can say more than words.

3.2

  Hi there.
1. This is Don.
2. Good morning, everyone.
3. I have a question.

UNIT 2

1.1

Paula: Hi, Dawn. I love your skirt. It looks great on you.

Dawn: Thanks. Guess what! I made this skirt myself from materials I recycled. . . . I like to buy used clothes in second-hand stores[1] and recycle them. I made this skirt from an old cotton shirt. Does that make sense? I also use old jeans to make skirts.

Paula: Really? Well, I like to recycle clothes, too, but I don't make clothes. I donate my old clothes to thrift stores. Then people like you can buy my old clothes. I don't like to throw clothes in the trash.

1.2

Paula: Hi, Dawn. I love your skirt. It looks great on you.

Dawn: Thanks. Guess what! I made this skirt myself from materials I recycled. . . . I like to buy used clothes in second-hand stores and recycle them. I made this skirt from an old cotton shirt. Does that make sense? I also use old jeans to make skirts.

Paula: Really? Well, I like to recycle clothes, too, but I don't make clothes. I donate my old clothes to thrift stores. Then people like you can buy my old clothes. I don't like to throw clothes in the trash.

Dawn: That's a great thing to do. Do you know that recycled clothing is a trend around the world? Even some famous people are wearing recycled clothes. The other day, Angelina Jolie was on TV and she was wearing a dress made from recycled materials. It fit her perfectly!

Paula: Wow! That's really interesting. So, what else do you make from recycled clothes?

Dawn: I make a lot of unusual things from old clothes. One time I made a pair of shoes from some old belts. They were fun to make, but they weren't very comfortable. I also make

---

[1]**second-hand stores:** stores that sell used goods, like clothes, at low prices

things from organic materials like cotton and wool. Right now I'm making a purse from old shirts and blankets. See?

Paula: Interesting! Do you make gifts for your friends? You know, my birthday is next month . . .

1.4

Interviewer: Today, we're talking with Deborah Lindquist, a famous eco-fashion designer in Los Angeles. Let's start with a basic question. What is eco-fashion?

Lindquist: Eco-fashion is fashion that uses organic materials like wool and cotton. I use organic materials in my eco-fashion, but I also recycle clothes—so for example, I use old saris and kimonos—to make new and unusual clothing.

Interviewer: Saris and Kimonos?

Lindquist: Yes, you know, saris are the beautiful, colorful clothes that women wear in India. And kimonos are the robes that women wear in Japan.

Interviewer: Wow—interesting. I bet the clothes you make are beautiful. So, what other materials do you use?

Lindquist: I use a lot of vintage[1] materials—beautiful materials from the 1940s.

UNIT 3

1.1

Host: We're continuing our talk about rap music this afternoon. Yesterday you heard a record producer and a professor of education give their opinions about rap music. Today you'll hear from Ms. Jones, the mother of two teenage boys, and Rashawn, a 16-year-old fan of rap music.

1.2

Host: We're continuing our talk about rap music this afternoon. Yesterday you heard a record producer and a professor of education give their opinions about rap music. Today you'll hear from Ms. Jones, the mother of two teenage boys, and Rashawn, a 16-year-old fan of rap music.

Ms. Jones, you have a strong opinion about rap music.

Ms. Jones: That's right. I live in a poor neighborhood where almost fifty percent of the boys don't finish high school. Many of them just don't see why education is important.

Host: That might be surprising to some of our listeners, but what does it have to do with rap music?

Ms. Jones: Well, I think that rappers are a bad example for our kids. Most of these rappers probably never finished school, and now they're rich and famous. If you listen to their songs, all you hear about is how great it is to have so much money. And in the videos all you see are men wearing gold jewelry. I don't want my boys to think, well, if I were

like them I could be rich too. It makes them think school's not important.

Rashawn: Whoa! You got it all wrong. We don't even listen to the words. It's all about the rhythm. If you ask me, these guys set a good example. Almost no one around here finishes school and goes to college. And if they do, as soon as they get a job, they're gone. They get out of this neighborhood as fast as they can. But the rappers don't forget about where they came from. And their songs are about us.

Host: Well, the two of you have very different opinions. But how about rap as a popular form of music? Do you have anything to say about the music itself?

Ms. Jones: What music? There's no melody, they don't play any musical instruments. If you ask me, this isn't even music.

Rashawn: But it's our own kind of music. It's not about melody. It's about language.

Ms. Jones: Language? It's just a lot of slang . . .

Rashawn: Yeah, it's slang to you, but this is the way we talk. The art is to find words that rhyme and to keep the rhythm going.

Host: Well, this is very interesting, I wish we could continue. But I'm afraid that's all we have time for today.

1.3

The principal of Washington High School invited two people to speak to the Parents' Organization about rap music: Mr. Robbie Simon, a successful music producer, and Professor Brad Crosby, a professor of education.

Principal: Thank you for speaking to our Parents' Organization this evening. I think we all know that rap music is very popular, but, as you know, some parents think that rap is bad. They don't like the words in rap songs, and they don't like what the songs say. Some of them even say that rap isn't real music because the songs have no melody and the rappers don't play any instruments. So they don't want their children to listen to rap music. Mr. Simon, what can you say to these parents?

Mr. Simon: Well, first I want to say that rap music started more than thirty years ago, and it is still very popular today. So, how can people say, "Rap is bad"? In my opinion, a lot of parents don't understand rap music. That's the real problem! Rap is very different from the music that most parents listen to. That's why they think rap is bad. They just can't understand it.

Principal: Professor Crosby, do you agree?

Professor Crosby: No, I do not. I think parents today believe that rap music is bad for a very important reason. Let me explain: Most teenagers think that rappers are cool, so they want to copy them. So, a lot of teens wear hip-hop style clothes and they copy the rappers' language—you know, they use slang and bad words. And then, when they hear rap songs about guns or drugs or sex, they think those

---

[1]**vintage:** old and showing high quality

things are cool, too. And sometimes they copy what the rappers do, and then they can have a lot of big problems!

Mr. Simon: Oh, come on, Professor! Rap songs tell about real things in the rappers' lives, but they don't say that those things are good! If you ask me, parents have to teach their children what's good and what's bad—not rappers!

Principal: I'd like to say something. We have to remember that there are many different kinds of rap music. All rap is not "gangsta rap"—about guns and killing, like a lot of Tupac Shakur's music. Some rappers, like. . . . uh. . . . Kanye West, for example, don't talk about bad things. And Professor Crosby, you probably know that some teachers use rap music in elementary schools.

Professor Crosby: Yes, that's true. Some teachers use rap to teach math to young children. The rhythm of the music helps the children to learn and remember more.

Principal: Thank you both for speaking here tonight. I think the discussion about rap will continue for a long time.

UNIT 4

1.1

Narrator: Emeralds . . . beautiful, valuable, lucky. Emeralds are gorgeous green gemstones. You can see one of the largest emeralds, the Mogul Emerald, at the New York Museum of Natural History right now. It is huge. It is 217 carats and is worth a fortune. How do we know that it is so valuable?

1.2

Narrator: Emeralds . . . beautiful, valuable, lucky. Emeralds are gorgeous green gemstones. You can see one of the largest emeralds, the Mogul Emerald, at the New York Museum of Natural History right now. It is huge. It is 217 carats and is worth a fortune. How do we know that it is so valuable?

The four Cs—color, clarity, cut, and carat—tell us the value of emeralds. Color is the most important. Dark emeralds are worth more than light emeralds. The Mogul Emerald has the color, clarity, cut, and carat of an excellent emerald. It has a dark green color, and it appears to sparkle.

The Mogul Emerald has a fascinating history. It comes from India, and it is more than 300 years old. In 2001, an Indian art sale advertised the emerald, and a very wealthy person bought it for $2.2 million. Some people say this person is selfish. They say the emerald should be in a museum for everyone to see, not in someone's house. Well, now the Mogul Emerald is on display . . . at the Museum of Natural History! The owner of the emerald is doing the right thing and giving the emerald to the Museum of Natural History, but for a short time only. So come to the museum today, see the beautiful Mogul Emerald, and learn why it has a tradition of being lucky.

1.3

Tour Guide: Here we are—the Hope Diamond. Millions of people come to see this diamond every year. It's the most valuable diamond in the world.

Katelyn: How much is it worth?

Tour Guide: The Hope Diamond is worth 250 million dollars.

Crowd: Wow!

Tour Guide: Yes, it's the most valuable diamond in the world, but that's not all. This diamond has a fascinating history.

Bob: Is this the diamond that what's-his-name bought for what's-her-name? You know—the famous movie star's diamond?

Tour Guide: No. King Louis the XIV of France owned this diamond. Imagine . . . it's 1668 and you are Louis the XIV. A man comes to you from India with a huge blue diamond. It is 112 carats! You buy it from him and your jeweler cuts it so it's very beautiful and it sparkles. Now it's 67 carats, and this beautiful jewel is called the "Blue Diamond of the Crown."

Katelyn: Oh, I think I know the rest of the story. Somebody steals it, right?

Tour Guide: Yes. In 1792, somebody steals it and it's gone for a long, long time. Then it appears in London, but it's cut down to 44 carats. It's smaller, but it still has that beautiful clear blue color. Then a wealthy man buys it. His name is Henry Philip Hope, and that's why we call it the Hope Diamond.

UNIT 5

1.1

John Shaw: Hi, everyone. Welcome to the Alzheimer's Organization. My name is John Shaw and I'm the president of the organization's poetry club. Why is this club special? It is special because it offers people with Alzheimer's disease the opportunity to get together and read poems to each other. We meet two times each month. I hope your relatives with Alzheimer's will want to join.

1.2

John Shaw: Hi, everyone. Welcome to the Alzheimer's Organization. My name is John Shaw and I'm the president of the organization's poetry club. Why is this club special? It is special because it offers people with Alzheimer's disease the opportunity to get together and read poems to each other. We meet two times each month. I hope your relatives with Alzheimer's will want to join.

Relative 1: Excuse me. I have a question. Do they write the poems themselves?

John Shaw: They may, but they don't have to. They can bring in any poems they want to read.

Relative 2: My mother needs medical help all the time. How can other people with Alzheimer's help her?

John Shaw: Actually, the group members can help one another. They read together. Sometimes they need to help one another remember words. Your mother won't be on her own.

Relative 2: Ah, I see. It seems like it's a good way for the members to make friends, too.

John Shaw: Absolutely. They make friends and new memories. And they don't feel lonely anymore. Many people with Alzheimer's are very sad, but in our group, they are happy. They hang out together. They laugh and have fun. They want to come back every week.

Relative 1: That's wonderful. Is it true that reading poetry can help people with Alzheimer's remember their pasts?

John Shaw: Yes, sometimes poetry does help. One of my group members read a poem about Italy. Then he told me about the time he and his son got lost in Rome many years ago. They were in Rome for vacation. His son was there with me, listening to his father's story. He said that he remembered the story almost perfectly. And he told it all by himself.

Relative 2: How can my mother join your group? I think she'll like this very much.

1.3

Dr. Dienstag: Thank you, Ms. Oliver. Hello, everyone. Yes, my new group *is* a writers' group, and it *really is* for people with Alzheimer's. The members of my group get together once a week, and they write stories together.

Relative 1: Excuse me, did you say they write stories?

Dr. Dienstag: Yes, they write stories about their memories. Then they read their stories to the group, and we all talk about them.

Relative 2: Sorry, but . . . my father sometimes doesn't remember my name. How can writing a story help him?

Dr. Dienstag: That's a good question. You see, there are so many things that people with Alzheimer's can't do anymore. You know. . . . like work, or drive, or. . . . well, a lot of things. But many of them can remember their past very well. So, if they can remember something that happened a long time ago and write a story about it, they feel happy.

3.2

Alison's father is sick and needs help all the time. Help
1. He cannot make his own food any more. Make
2. He spends most of the time in bed. Bed
3. He asks about his wife again and again. Again
4. Alison is often at his place. Place
5. She visits him every day. Day
6. She hopes her father will get better. Better

UNIT 6

1.1

Dr. Kim: Today we'll talk about starting a new business. First, you must decide what to sell. Any ideas?

Student 1: You have to be creative and come up with something new.

Dr. Kim: Well, that's not easy to do.

Student 1: Really? Why not?

1.2

Dr. Kim: Today we'll talk about starting a new business. First, you must decide what to sell. Any ideas?

Student 1: You have to be creative and come up with something new.

Dr. Kim: Well, that's not easy to do.

Student 1: Really? Why not?

Dr. Kim: One reason is that it isn't easy to sell someone a new product. For example, maybe you make a bicycle, but it has four wheels and you can get around more quickly. People might think, "I already have a bicycle. I don't need a bike with this new feature."

Student 1: Oh, I see.

Dr. Kim: And there's another important reason why it's hard to come up with a new idea. Creativity. It's not easy to think of something that people don't already have.

Student 2: Have you heard of this new pencil called Write Forever? You never need to sharpen it. You can use it forever. A boy named Martin Green came up with this idea. People really liked it, and now Martin is the owner of a successful company.

Student 1: Wow! That's amazing!

Dr. Kim: That's a good example to discuss. Martin was only twelve years old. He had no business experience. But he had a creative idea and started an exciting new business.

Student 2: Only twelve years old? That's incredible.

Dr. Kim: Often kids are more creative than adults. As people get older, it's more difficult to be creative.

Student 1: Yeah, when I was a kid I had lots of creative new ideas. Now I'm kind of afraid to try anything new. I guess I think that I'll make a mistake.

Dr. Kim: Also when you're older, you don't have any free time. You're always working. To improve creativity, you need to relax.

Student 2: Right, relax.

Student 1: I have so much work. How can I relax?

Dr. Kim: First, never bring work home with you. When you finish work, don't think about it. Try to think like a kid, rather than an adult. There are other things you can do too, but let's get back to our discussion.

1.2, Question 6

Dr. Kim: Also when you're older, you don't have any free time. You're always working. To improve creativity, you need to relax.

Student 2: Right, relax.

1.3

Professor Ray: OK, everybody . . . what can we learn from K-K Gregory? First of all, she found something that she needed and other people needed, too. Second, she listened to other people. Her friends liked Wristies, her mother liked them . . . That's important. You have to talk to people. And then, she decided to start a business. She didn't know anything about business, but she wasn't afraid to try something completely new. Think about this, because this is very important: Children think they can do anything—and sometimes they can—because they aren't afraid! You know what our problem is? We're not children anymore! So we are afraid, we're always afraid to make mistakes! In school, at our jobs, making mistakes is bad, right?

Students: Yeah, sure, right . . .

Professor Ray: OK, so then what happens? We don't want to make mistakes, so we stop being creative. We forget how to be creative. But—we can remember how to be creative again. We can—*if* we can remember the feeling of being a child. Now, how do we do that? Well, there are many ways, but one way that I like is to meditate.

Students: What? Meditate? Huh? Really? OK . . .

Professor Ray: So let's try it. OK, now, everybody close your eyes . . . Everybody! Come on . . . Relax . . . relax. Now, think about when you were a child . . . Maybe you were 7, or 10, or 11 . . . Think about a time that you did something new . . . you tried something for the first time . . . and you weren't afraid . . . You did it . . . and you felt so good . . . Try to remember that good feeling . . . Take your time . . . just think . . . When you remember something, open your eyes, and then tell your story to another student. When you're finished, we'll discuss your stories together.

UNIT 7

1.1

Jackie: Hi, Naomi. Are you ready for the presentation?

Naomi: Yeah. I read about a woman named Ruth Davidow. She didn't get a Nobel Peace Prize, but she was an amazing woman.

1.2

Jackie: Hi, Naomi. Are you ready for the presentation?

Naomi: Yeah. I read about a woman named Ruth Davidow. She didn't get a Nobel Peace Prize, but she was an amazing woman. She came to the United States from Russia when she was three. She went to school and became a nurse.

Jackie: OK, so why are you going to talk about her?

Naomi: Well, she worked as a nurse to help fight for democracy in Spain.

Jackie: Huh? Why did she go to Spain?

Naomi: There was a war from 1936 to 1939 in Spain. About 3,000 Americans went to fight in the Spanish Civil War because they were against Franco. He was a dictator who finally won the war.

Jackie: Did the United States fight in the Spanish Civil War?

Naomi: No, the government didn't speak out about the violence in Spain. But the 3,000 Americans who had courage and went to Spain were called "the Abraham Lincoln Brigade." They fought for the Spanish people because they stood up for democracy.

Jackie: Wow. Were many people hurt?

Naomi: About 900 Americans in the Abraham Lincoln Brigade got killed. Ruth Davidow was shocked at the violence. She said, "I saw terrible things. The kinds of things we should never forget—kids of fifteen . . . being killed."

Jackie: What did she do when she came back to the United States?

Naomi: She continued to protest against injustice. After the Spanish Civil War, she said, "I can't live in the world if I can't fight against injustice." In 1965 she was a part of the Civil Rights Movement in the United States.

Jackie: The Civil Rights Movement was a political fight to get equal rights for African Americans, wasn't it?

Naomi: Yes. Ruth Davidow cared about so many important problems. She worked for women's right, too. And when she was 85, she was at the Third International Women's Conference in Beijing.

Jackie: She really had an interesting life.

Naomi: And a long life. She lived to be 88 years old.

1.3

Ruth: Wow, that was a great TV show! Wangari Maathai is an amazing woman. Your class presentation is going to be great.

Sara: Thanks. Who did you choose for your presentation?

Ruth: I picked Rigoberta Menchu Tum. She's from Guatemala.

Sara: Who is she? I've never heard of her.

Ruth: She's a leader for equal rights. She works to get equal rights for poor people in Guatemala, especially the Mayan people.

Sara: The Mayan people?

Ruth: Yeah. The Mayans are the native people in Central America. And a lot of them are very poor. Rigoberta Menchu Tum helps them and she also helps all women to get equal rights.

Sara: Oh . . . I think I read something about her. Did she win the Nobel Peace Prize?

Ruth: Yeah, in 1992. She was the first native person in the world to win the Peace Prize. And she did all of this without any education.

Sara: Really?

Ruth: Yes. She went to elementary school in the countryside, but just for a very short time. Her family was so poor they needed her to work in their fields. She left school when she was only eight years old. After that, she continued to study, but she did it all on her own.

Sara: That's incredible. How did she become an important leader?

Ruth: Well, when Rigoberta was a teenager, she and her family joined a political organization. They wanted to help poor workers. And they wanted to change the government. They wanted a democracy.

Sara: What happened?

Ruth: Well, of course the government wanted to stop that political group. So they put Rigoberta's whole family in jail—her father, her mother, and her brother—and they beat them up. And then later, they killed all of them.

Sara: Oh, how horrible! What happened to Rigoberta?

Ruth: Well, the government wanted to put her in jail, too, so she left Guatemala and she went to Mexico.

Sara: What did she do in Mexico?

Ruth: There were other Guatemalan people there at that time. So, Rigoberta worked with them to bring a democratic government to Guatemala.

Sara: Wow . . . what an incredible woman.

Ruth: Yeah, she became a very important political leader in Guatemala. And even though the government killed her whole family, she never encouraged people to use violence. In her Nobel Peace Prize speech, she said, "We have learned that change cannot come through war."

Sara: Wow, I can understand why she won the Nobel Peace Prize.

Ruth: I know! And listen to this . . . Here it is . . . The Nobel Committee said Rigoberta's life is a "shining example of non-violence." They said she is an example for the whole world to follow.

Sara: That's beautiful. You know, Ribogerta and Wangari Maathai are similar in a lot of ways.

Ruth: Yeah, you're right. We both picked good women to talk about in class!

UNIT 8

1.1

Dr: So, Mr. Hansen, why have you come to talk to me?

Mr. Hansen: Believe me, I'd rather not be here. But I've been to traffic school twice. That didn't help, so they said I needed to see a psychologist or they'd take my driver's license away.

Dr: I see. So you have a problem controlling your anger.

1.2

Dr.: So, Mr. Hansen, why have you come to talk to me?

Mr. Hansen: Believe me, I'd rather not be here. But I've been to traffic school twice. That didn't help, so they said I needed to see a psychologist or they'd take my driver's license away.

Dr.: I see. So you have a problem controlling your anger.

Mr. Hansen: *Wait a minute.* I don't think I have a problem. Just because I'm not always polite, I am not a rude driver.

Dr.: So why did you have to go to traffic school?

Mr. Hansen: The first time, I was waiting at an intersection when the light turned green. I was in a hurry, and the guy in front of me didn't go. So I honked and started yelling at him.

Dr.: Well *hold on a minute,* don't you think that's rude behavior?

Mr. Hansen: Not at all. The guy wasn't paying attention.

Dr.: Hmm, I think this is going to be difficult. Pretend you were the man in that car. Maybe you were thinking about an argument you had had that morning with your wife.

Mr. Hansen: That's his problem.

Dr.: Oh dear. This is going to be even harder than I thought. How about the second time you were in traffic school? Why did you have to go then?

Mr. Hansen: I have no idea.

Dr.: Really? The traffic school sent me a report about you. They say that you were tailgating. What about this?

Mr. Hansen: Not my problem. The freeway was crowded. I was in a hurry so I changed lanes. I was in the fast lane and the car in front of me was too slow.

Dr.: Mr. Hansen, let's try a role play. You are driving on the freeway. You're going to work.

Mr. Hansen: OK. I'm driving on the freeway, and I'm twenty minutes late.

Dr.: No, no, no. You are very calm. I'm driving, and I'm mad because I'm late to work. I drive right up to your tailgate and honk at you. How does that make you feel?

Mr. Hansen: Well, I think to myself, I'm going too slowly. That guy is right. I should get out of his way.

Dr.: OK, Mr. Hansen, I can't help you.

1.2, Question 5

Mr. Hansen: The first time, I was waiting at an intersection when the light turned green. I was in a hurry and the guy in front of me didn't go. So I honked and started yelling at him.

Dr.: Well *hold on a minute,* don't you think that's rude behavior?

Mr. Hansen: Not at all. The guy wasn't paying attention.

Dr.: Hmm, I think this is going to be difficult. Pretend you were the man in that car. Maybe you were thinking about an argument you had that morning with your wife.

Mr. Hansen: That's his problem.

1.3

Psychologist: Come on, Allen. You can do it. We talked about this. You know what to do.

Allen: I know. I know what to do, but I just can't do it.

Psychologist: Now what is it, Allen? What exactly are you scared of?

Allen: I don't know. I just hate crossing the bridge. I don't want to do it.

Psychologist: Come on, Allen. You can do it. Think of all the other things you do: your job, your sports, your music. You're very good at everything you do. You can do this, too.

Allen: Too many trucks.

Psychologist: What did you say?

Allen: I'm scared of the trucks! The trucks are going to hit me!

Psychologist: They're not going to hit you, Allen. Don't look at the trucks. The best thing to do is just look at the road.

Allen: I can't. There's too much water! What if we fall?

Psychologist: Don't think of the water, Allen. Just look at the road. Look straight ahead.

Allen: Oh no, we're on the bridge!

Psychologist: Keep looking at the road, Allen. Look straight ahead. You're doing fine. Keep going. You're doing fine. There! You did it! You crossed the bridge!

Allen: *We* crossed the bridge. I can't do it alone.

Psychologist: You will, Allen. You will. Now keep going . . .

UNIT 9

1.1

Maria Sanchez: Welcome back to "Changing Families." I'm Maria Sanchez. Today we're going to talk to children who have siblings. Some studies show that children who have siblings are happier than only children. They show that they are less selfish and not as spoiled as only children. Let's hear what two children have to say.

1.2

Maria Sanchez: Welcome back to "Changing Families." I'm Maria Sanchez. Today we're going to talk to children who have siblings. Some studies show that children who have siblings are happier than only children. They show that they are less selfish and not as spoiled as only children. Let's hear what two children have to say. First, I'm going to talk to Alicia.

Hi, Alicia. Do you have brothers and sisters?

Alicia: I have two brothers.

Maria Sanchez: Oh, that's nice. You have kids you can play with.

Alicia: Well, yes. But they like to be with their friends. And sometimes we don't get along with each other.

Maria: Oh, how does that make you feel?

Alicia: Sometimes I feel lonely. I told my mom and dad that I want a little sister. Mom said three kids are enough. And Dad said we can't afford any more kids.

Maria: Well, I had two brothers, also. And when I got older, I was glad I had brothers. But I know how you feel. Now I'm going to talk to Vincent.

Vincent, how many brothers and sisters do you have?

Vincent: Two brothers and two sisters.

Maria: Wow! That's a big family, especially now. You don't ever feel alone, I guess.

Vincent: No way!

Maria: You're the oldest, right?

Vincent: Yeah.

Maria: So you have to help take care of your siblings, I bet.

Vincent: Yeah. Both my parents work. They're pretty tired when they get home, so I help raise the other kids.

Maria: That's a big job for a 15-year-old.

Vincent: Yeah. I think it makes me self-confident, though. I'm really glad I have a large family.

Maria: I agree. You seem very self-confident. Thank you for talking with us on "Changing Families."

1.3

Maria Sanchez: Welcome back. What do kids think about being an only child? Let's find out right now! I'm going to speak to Marion and Mark's daughter, Tonia, and to Tom and Jenna's son, Jay. Hi, Tonia.

Tonia: Hi.

Maria: How old are you, sweetheart?

Tonia: Eight.

Maria: Eight. And Jay, you are . . . ?

Jay: I'm thirteen.

Maria: OK. Now Tonia, you're the only child in your family, right?

Tonia: Uh-huh.

Maria: And is that OK with you?

Tonia: No! I hate it . . .

Maria: Really . . . Why?

Tonia: Because I want a sister.

Maria: Oh . . .

Tonia: All my friends have brothers and sisters. I'm the only kid in my class who doesn't have one!

Maria: Oh, I see . . . um . . . Did you ever talk to your mom and dad about it?

Tonia: Yeah, I talked to my mom.

Maria: And what did she say?

Tonia: She said, "I am 46 years old. I am not going to have another child."

Maria: And how did you feel then?

Tonia: I was sad.

Maria: But can you understand your mom and dad?

Tonia: Yeah.

Maria: Well, that's good.

Tonia: But I still want a sister!

Maria: Well, here's a little girl who knows what she wants! Thanks, Tonia. And Jay, how about you? Do you feel the same way?

Jay: No, not at all. I like my family like this.

Maria: Mmhm . . . But do you ever feel lonely?

Jay: No, I don't feel lonely. I feel special! I do a lot of things together with my parents. We always have fun together.

Maria: What kinds of things do you do with your parents?

Jay: Well, the best thing is that we travel a lot. Like, last year, we went to Europe. And this winter, we're going to go skiing in Colorado.

Maria: Wow, that's great!

Jay: Yeah, and I think it's easier for us to do all of these things because it's just the three of us.

Maria: You mean, because your parents can afford it, right?

Jay: Yes, uh-huh . . .

Maria: But do you ever feel different from your friends?

Jay: No. Actually, a lot of my friends are only children, too.

Maria: How interesting . . . Thanks Jay, and thanks to you, too, Tonia.

Tonia and **Jay:** You're welcome.

Maria: Well, there you have it—two children, and two very different opinions about being an only child. Thanks for watching!

UNIT 10

1.1

John Martin: Hello, this is John Martin, your host on *Sports Line*. Today we're taking calls from sports fans around the world. Tell us about the national sport of your country.

1.2

John Martin: Hello, this is John Martin, your host on *Sports Line*. Today we're taking calls from sports fans around the world. Tell us about the national sport of your country.

Our first caller is James from the United Kingdom.

James: Hello. Yes, well of course soccer is the universal sport. But in England, rugby is also a national sport. Unfortunately, even though I love a good rugby match, I rarely go anymore. It's gotten quite expensive, you see. We really should try to keep our national sport alive.

John: Yes, that is so true. Our next caller is Jean-Pierre, from Paris.

Jean-Pierre: As you know, our national soccer team is the best in the world. Soccer is the only sport for us. Every neighborhood has a soccer field and all kids play this sport. Of course, we know about baseball. What a boring sport! A soccer match is much more exciting even though the scores of most games are not very high. If your nationality is French, your game is soccer.

John: OK, then. Let's hear from Soledad in Madrid.

Soledad: It's amazing! I agree with the French about something. Baseball is boring. For us, soccer is the perfect sport. It's easy for kids to learn. There's no equipment except a soccer ball and a goal. But in our history bullfighting was our national sport. It's a pity people think it's so cruel. Everyone should see bullfighting. Then they will understand the beauty of this sport.

John: OK, we're out of time. Please send us an e-mail. Tell us what your favorite sport is.

1.3

Commentator: Welcome to *America Talks*. We are taking calls from sports fans all over the country this morning. We want to hear your opinions about soccer: Why isn't soccer popular in the United States? The World Cup is happening right now. About 700 million people all over the world are going to watch the final match on television. But many Americans, even sports fans, do not even know that it's happening. How can Americans NOT be interested in a game that the rest of the world loves—a game that is universal?

Our first caller is Bob from Kearny, New Jersey. Welcome to the show, Bob.

Bob: Thanks for taking my call.

Commentator: Bob, why isn't soccer popular in this country?

Bob: Well, I think it's mostly because of the score. You can have a great soccer match, but the final score can be zero to one. I think Americans like to see high scores—they like the numbers to say more about the teams.

Commentator: Interesting point. People also say that ties are a problem for sports fans in the U.S. We really like to have a winner.

Bob: Yeah, I agree.

Commentator: Thanks for the call, Bob. Next, we have Steve from Rochester, New York, on the line. Hello, Steve.

Steve: Hi. You know, I think the main reason soccer isn't popular here is that most of us just didn't grow up with it. Maybe we played a little when we were kids, but we never watched it on TV or listened to it on the radio with our families.

Commentator: So you think the problem is that soccer is not a tradition in this country?

Steve: Yeah. Our traditions in the U.S. are baseball, football, and basketball. If you watch all three of those sports, you're pretty busy. You don't really need another sport.

Commentator: Thanks for your comments, Steve. We have one more call, from Drew in Seattle, Washington. Go ahead, Drew.

Drew: Well, you know Americans love stars. But we haven't had any really big soccer stars here yet. Pele came to play in the U.S. in 1975, and he was a star on the field, but not off the field. And that was a long time ago. Some people say David Beckham is going to get Americans interested in soccer. He IS a star—both on the field and off. He has the Hollywood life. He really might help soccer in the U.S.

Commentator: Yes, I've heard that, too. It could happen. I guess we'll see. Thanks for your call, Drew.

Achievement Tests Answer Key

UNIT 1

1.1

B

1.2

1. A   2. C   3. B   4. D   5. D   6. B

1.3

1. B   2. F   3. A

2.1

1. interested in   6. make
2. application   7. international
3. stay   8. spend
4. travelled   9. culture
5. lazy   10. happy

3.1

1. is   3. are   5. was
2. am   4. was

3.2

1. A   2. C   3. D

3.3

1. Where did you live?
2. Did you have problems speaking with them?

4.1

Answers will vary. Possible answer:
Can you explain why you had time to travel?

4.2

Answers will vary. Possible answer:
Don is friendly and hardworking.

4.3

Answers will vary. See the scoring rubric on page T-72.

UNIT 2

1.1

D

1.2

1. B   2. B   3. D

1.3

shoes, skirts, dresses

1.4

1. F   2. A   3. B

2.1

1. materials   4. unusual
2. trash   5. famous
3. environment

2.2

1. C   2. F   3. B   4. A   5. E

3.1

1. are looking   3. is wearing
2. am going   4. am making

3.2

1. 2   2. 3   3. 3   4. 2

3.3

Got it?; Any questions?

4.1

Answers will vary. Possible answers:
Does that make sense?, See?

4.2

It means that you're wearing formal or special clothes
(not everyday clothing).

4.3

Answers will vary. See the scoring rubric on page T-72.

UNIT 3

1.1

C

1.2

1. D   2. B   3. B   4. A   5. C   6. B

1.3

Professor Crosby: C
Ms. Jones: E
Rashawn: D

2.1

1. popular   4. instruments
2. melody   5. play
3. rhyme

2.2

1. D   2. C   3. A   4. B   5. A

3.1

1. A   2. A   3. B   4. A

3.2

1. A   2. A   3. B

3.3

1. A   2. B   3. A

4.1

B. Rashawn

4.2

Answers will vary. Possible answer:
In my opinion, rap music is good because it is easy to dance to.

4.3

Answers will vary. See the scoring rubric on page T-72.

UNIT 4

1.1

C

1.2

1. B   3. B   5. A   7. D
2. B   4. A   6. C

1.3

1. D. The Hope Diamond
2. E. The Mogul Emerald

2.1

1. huge   3. wealthy   5. steal
2. valuable   4. worth

2.2

1. G   2. A   3. E   4. C   5. D

3.1

1. gets
2. Does [your wife] like
3. does not wear OR doesn't wear
4. sparkles
5. does [it] cost

3.2

1. C   2. A   3. C   4. C   5. B

4.1

Answers will vary.

4.2

Answers will vary.

4.3

Answers will vary. See the scoring rubric on page T-72.

UNIT 5

1.1

B

1.2

1. C   2. D   3. B   4. D   5. A   6. D

1.3

D, E, F

2.1

1. by yourself   3. with friends
2. on my own   4. make new friends

2.2

1. F   2. H   3. B   4. E   5. D   6. C

3.1

1. do you like to do
2. does not want to help OR doesn't want to help
3. want to get
4. does Jim need to buy

3.2

1. /ey/   2. /ɛ/   3. /ɛ/   4. /ey/   5. /ey/   6. /ɛ/

4.1

Answers will vary. Possible answer:
The poetry club helps people to make friends.

4.2

Answers will vary.

4.3

Answers will vary. See the scoring rubric on page T-72.

UNIT 6

1.1

A

1.2

1. C   2. D   3. C   4. D   5. A   6. C

1.3

1. C   2. D   3. B

2.1

1. exciting   4. work experience
2. come up with   5. owner
3. improve creativity

2.2

1. A   2. C   3. A   4. B   5. D

3.1

1. There was
2. there were
3. Are there
4. there are

3.2

1. A
2. B
3. A

3.3

1. B
2. C
3. B

4.1

Answers may vary. Possible answers:
Write Forever, a new pencil, a special pencil, a pencil

4.2

Answers will vary. Possible answer:
That's interesting;

4.3

Answers will vary. See the scoring rubric on page T-72.

UNIT 7

1.1

B

1.2

1. A
2. B
3. B
4. C
5. B
6. D

1.3

1. E
2. B
3. F

2.1

1. democracy
2. protest against
3. had courage
4. stood up for
5. violence
6. shocked

2.2

1. A
2. D
3. B
4. A

3.1

1. spoke
2. Did he fight
3. learned
4. didn't believe

3.2

1. C
2. C
3. B

3.3

1. D
2. A
3. C

4.1

Answers will vary. Possible answer:
Ruth Davidow fought for democracy.

4.2

Answers will vary. Possible answer:
Rigoberta Menchu fought for democracy, and Ruth Davidow did, too.

4.3

Answers will vary. See the scoring rubric on page T-72.

UNIT 8

1.1

C

1.2

1. C
2. B
3. A
4. A
5. B
6. C

1.3

1. E
2. F
3. A

2.1

1. control
2. rude
3. psychologist
4. intersection
5. paying attention
6. honks
7. polite
8. crowded
9. lane
10. tailgating

3.1

1. did not see OR didn't see
2. was paying attention
3. was talking
4. hit

3.2

1. A
2. B
3. C
4. B
5. B
6. A

4.1

Answers will vary. Possible answer:
The person driving the car in front of him didn't go when the light turned green.

4.2

Answers will vary. Possible answer:
Well, I still think you should be polite on the road.

4.3

Answers will vary. See the scoring rubric on page T-72.

UNIT 9

1.1

C

1.2

1. D
2. C
3. B
4. A
5. C
6. A

1.3

Tonia: F

Jay and Vincent: D

Tonia and Alicia: E

2.1

1. afford
2. take care of
3. siblings
4. spoiled
5. get along with

2.2

1. A 2. D 3. A 4. B 5. A

3.1

1. It's (it is) going to be
2. Are you going to have
3. we're not
4. is going to start

3.2

1. B 2. B 3. A

3.3

1. B 2. C 3. A

4.1

B

4.2

Answers will vary. Possible answer:

That's for sure. I agree that children with siblings are less selfish.

4.3

Answers will vary. See the scoring rubric on page T-72.

UNIT 10

1.1

D

1.2

1. B 2. B 3. C 4. A 5. D 6. A

1.3

1. D 2. B 3. F

2.1

1. universal
2. fans
3. team
4. match
5. nationalities

2.2

1. C 2. A 3. A 4. B 5. D

3.1

1. It should not be very important to score a lot of points.
2. Americans should watch more soccer.
3. You should wear the right clothes to play soccer.
4. A sport should be fun to play.

3.2

1. A 2. C 3. A

3.3

1. A 2. B 3. B

4.1

They think that baseball is boring.

4.2

Answers will vary. Possible answers:

I don't like baseball because it is slow.

OR

I like baseball, so I watch it every night.

4.3

Answers will vary. See the scoring rubric on page T-72.

NorthStar 1 Achievement Test Scoring Rubric: Speaking

Score	Description
4	A response at this level demonstrates somewhat clear speech, with multiple short pauses and hesitations, and some correct pronunciation of words; a response at this level is also marked by: • generally accurate information with some connection to listening • some use of grammatical features such as prepositional phrases, modals, simple verb tenses, and direct objects • use of a few vocabulary words from unit • accurate use of most grammar and vocabulary
3	A response at this level demonstrates somewhat clear speech, with one or two long pauses and hesitations, and some correct pronunciation of words; a response at this level is also marked by: • general information that is somewhat connected to listening; information that needs more development • some inconsistent use of grammatical features such as pronouns, subject-verb agreement, and simple present verbs • reliance on several vocabulary words from prompt; recycled language • noticeable errors in grammar and vocabulary use
2	A response at this level attempts to address the prompt in English, and is marked by multiple long pauses, very slow speech, and limited correct pronunciation of words; a response at this level is also marked by: • general information that is vaguely connected to listening; information that needs to be developed significantly • use of few basic formulaic expressions • reliance on one or two vocabulary words from prompt; recycled words • frequent errors in grammar and vocabulary use
I	A response at this level attempts to address the prompt in English, and is marked by long periods of silence or unintelligible speech; a response at this level is also marked by: • the need to make connections with listening and develop that information • use of isolated words or short utterances • very limited range of vocabulary • frequent errors in grammar and vocabulary use
0	Speaker makes no attempt to respond OR speech is dominated by a foreign language.

Notes

Notes

Notes

CD Tracking Guide
Achievement Tests

Track	Activity	Page
1	Audio Program Introduction	
	UNIT 1	
2	Part 1: Listening 1.1	T-1
3	1.2	T-1
4	1.3	T-2
5	Part 3: Skills for Speaking 3.2	T-4
	UNIT 2	
6	Part 1: Listening 1.1	T-7
7	1.2	T-7
8	1.4	T-8
9	Part 3: Skills for Speaking 3.2	T-10
	UNIT 3	
10	Part 1: Listening 1.1	T-12
11	1.2	T-12
12	1.3	T-13
13	Part 3: Skills for Speaking 3.2	T-16
	UNIT 4	
14	Part 1: Listening 1.1	T-19
15	1.2	T-19
16	1.3	T-21
17	Part 3: Skills for Speaking 3.2	T-23
	UNIT 5	
18	Part 1: Listening 1.1	T-25
19	1.2	T-25
20	1.3	T-26
21	Part 3: Skills for Speaking 3.2	T-28

Track	Activity	Page
	UNIT 6	
22	Part 1: Listening 1.1	T-30
23	1.2	T-30
24	1.2, Question 6	T-31
25	1.3	T-31
26	Part 3: Skills for Speaking 3.2	T-34
	UNIT 7	
27	Part 1: Listening 1.1	T-36
28	1.2	T-36
29	1.3	T-37
30	Part 3: Skills for Speaking 3.2	T-39
	UNIT 8	
31	Part 1: Listening 1.1	T-42
32	1.2	T-42
33	1.2, Question 5	T-43
34	1.3	T-43
35	Part 3: Skills for Speaking 3.2	T-45
	UNIT 9	
36	Part 1: Listening 1.1	T-47
37	1.2	T-47
38	1.3	T-48
39	Part 3: Skills for Speaking 3.2	T-50
	UNIT 10	
40	Part 1: Listening 1.1	T-53
41	1.2	T-53
42	1.3	T-54
43	Part 3: Skills for Speaking 3.2	T-56